Girls will be Girls

By the same Author

NINETEEN TO THE DOZEN

Contents

INTRODUCTION	ix
GIRLS WILL BE GIRLS	1
A FORM OF FLATTERY	7
BEST-SELLERS OF THE CENTURY	12
(a) *The Rosary*	12
(b) *Tell England*	17
AN IMPORTANT FIND	22
CHRISTMAS REVIEWS OF BOOKS FOR GIRLS:	
1935 and 1936	26
LITERARY PITFALLS	32
(a) It Was A Night For Lovers . . .	32
(b) I First Saw The Light Of Day . . .	37
CHRISTMAS REVIEWS OF BOOKS FOR GIRLS:	
1937 and 1939	43
CRITIC'S CORNER: LADIES	49
Barbara Cartland	49
Christabel Aberconway	51
Mata Hari	52
Rosemary Brown	53
Marilyn Monroe	55
Norah Docker	56
Skittles	57
Aimee Semple McPherson	59
Edith Summerskill	60
Elsa Maxwell	62
Phyllis Bottome	64
The Queen Mother	65

Contents

THE CROOKED BAT	67
ERIC BROUGHT UP TO DATE	92
CHRISTMAS REVIEWS OF BOOKS FOR GIRLS: 1951	98
LATE VICTORIAN PREOCCUPATIONS	102
(a) Aerated Waters	102
(b) Cycling Roadsters	105
CHRISTMAS REVIEWS OF BOOKS FOR GIRLS: 1954 and 1955	109
CRITIC'S CORNER: GENTLEMEN	115
Serge Lifar	115
Billy Bunter	116
William McGonagall	117
Christiaan Barnard	119
Beverley Nichols	120
Montague Summers	123
Malcolm MacDonald	124
Donald Portway	126
Baba	127
Godfrey Winn	129
CHRISTMAS REVIEWS OF BOOKS FOR GIRLS: 1956 and 1957	133
JUST AN ORDINARY TERM	141
THE PLEASURES OF READING	143
Ethel M. Dell	143
A Clip of Steel	145
Dr. Bowdler	147
The Correspondence of Murder	149
The Mysterious Affair at The Pines	151
Pin-ups and Poetry	153
Jack the Ripper	155
Isadora Duncan	156
Woolfs' Lair	158

Contents

Mind Your Manners	160
Lillie Langtry	163
School Songs	164
Marmalade, Ma'am?	167
Elinor Glyn	170
CHRISTMAS REVIEWS OF BOOKS FOR GIRLS: 1959 and 1961	173

INTRODUCTION

A word of explanation...
From childhood on, I had always thought that schoolmistresses and schoolgirls were funny and in 1932, at the age of 22, I started to invent little turns and skits about them which I inflicted on startled guests at parties—headmistresses addressing the girls at the end of term, botany mistresses leading a nature ramble, and so on. In 1934, a BBC producer heard me and put me into a Charlot's Hour, a monthly late-hour entertainment on the wireless. It was thought piquant that a schoolmaster, as I then was, should be doing this sort of thing and I got a certain amount of publicity. I have been broadcasting on various subjects ever since.

In 1935, I started to make gramophone records of some of this material for Columbia and in the same year Raymond Mortimer, at that time literary editor of the *New Statesman*, asked me to review, in the Christmas books number, the large collection of schoolgirl stories that publishers sent in (Angela Brazil was still writing), and this happy yearly task continued until the war. In post-war years I branched out and was entrusted with books that did not only concern schoolgirls.

The book here before you consists mainly of excerpts from some of the activities named above. Bulk reading of reviews of schoolgirl stories would prove an indigestible diet and might be actually injurious to the health, so I have dotted them about in the text in, I hope, easily consumed portions. I have added the date of each item.

For allowing me to reprint the extracts, I am grateful to the BBC, the *New Statesman*, the *Listener*, the *Sunday Times*, the *Times Educational Supplement*, *Punch* and *The Observer*. And I shall ever be grateful to the late Dr. Kenneth Fisher, my headmaster at Oundle in 1934, for letting me absent myself from the

Introduction

classroom at regular intervals in order to broadcast. He, too, kindly thought it piquant. 'What are you up to *now*, you monkey?' was his usual greeting when I went in to his study to ask his permission. But for him, what I was, and am, up to might never have happened.

GIRLS WILL BE GIRLS

A broadcast in 1954

In case your surprised eyebrows should rise uncomfortably high at the prospect of being addressed on fiction for girls by a man, I had better explain my limited qualifications. For the past nineteen years, a weekly magazine whose name you would know well has kindly asked me to review each year a large Christmas batch of stories for girls. In this way I have been able to read much that is best of Angela Brazil, Dorita Fairlie Bruce, Winifred Darch, Bessie Marchant, May Wynne, and many others. I have read their works with absorption, amazement, delight, and with a reasonably straight face. I have lived with the characters and shared their emotions. I have shivered in my shoes when Mona Beaseley has gone shinning up the church spire. I have been as appalled as Miss Fortescue when the music master was discovered to be definitely in the pay of a Balkan Power. I have giggled at Mademoiselle as blithely as any junior, and I have been as breathless as Matron herself that day when circumstances forced her to trudgeon through the mill-race when Felicity Brownlow's water-wings got a puncture.

Of recent years, two increasingly popular subjects have complicated the lives of many fictional schoolgirls. They are both methods of locomotion. One is ponies, the other spaceships. Of these two ways of getting about, by far the more elaborate and unsatisfactory is pony-travel. Of course, there is much to be gained. Proficiency astride a pony leads in the end to the intoxicating day of the gymkhana when, in the upper-crust world inevitably connected with quadrupeds, Gloria Castleton gets rosette after rosette dished out to her by a titled lady, sporting for the occasion a dashing pair of cerise jodhpurs.

Girls will be Girls

But what a lot Gloria has to go through before she reaches that supreme moment. The details must baffle any but the most horsey reader. Gloria has to know just what and where are lunge reins, half passes, snaffles, dressage and pelhams. She has to know what to do for the best with curry combs, saddle soap, dandy brushes and cheek-straps. Did *you* know that a grey gelding of fourteen hands could possibly suffer from sweet-itch? Before so much as mounting her mettlesome steed, Gloria has to soak her tack in neat's-foot oil and be able to throw off sentences such as 'She has a lovely sloping shoulder, good withers and nice clean legs', or 'His impulsion is tremendous and I note that he's building up condition on his hocks'.

And then, the ponies themselves. Heaven knows what disasters cannot befall them! They can develop a thing called warbles, they can forget to change legs, they can be entered for the Handy Hunter Class and then run full tilt into a double-oxer. They can get their curb chains twisted clockwise, which appears to be fatal, they can work up a lather at a most awkward moment, they can get their bridoon tangled in their girths. Of course, Gloria and Snowball together manage all this successfully in the end, but the emotional strain on the reader is very great.

With space-ships, however, all is different. The important thing about these new-fangled contraptions is that nothing by any chance ever goes wrong. After a hearty, unhurried breakfast, Beryl and Brenda climb the ladder to the gleaming monster and step confidently inside. For the trip, they are usually tastefully arrayed in the latest thing in space-wear: a one-piece fawn coverall in a high-grade Shetland, with little ruchings here and there to ease the hardness of the lines. Sometimes they travel to the Moon just as they are in their gym-tunics, perhaps slipping on a pressure coatee to lessen the jolt at taking-off time.

A quick glance round the dials, an exploratory touch of the steering-wheel just to get the feel of the thing, and then we are ready. Brenda closes the door, Beryl sets the fins after a lightning peep at her logarithm tables, and then together they smartly press a button marked TO START, PRESS THE BUTTON. A shudder, a roar, and before they know where they are, they are gazing down at Bognor Regis from a height of 85,000

Girls will be Girls

miles. The first thing to do is to call up Mums on the radio telephone, dialling Edgbaston 459668. Mums never appears to be for one moment anxious. 'Have fun, darlings', she screams, or 'Pop on an extra woolly if it's chilly'. What Dads is thinking seldom emerges. Quite a lot, I should imagine.

Arrival at the Moon presents no sort of trouble. With their plastic breathing apparatuses working to perfection, Brenda and Beryl step lithely out, plant the school flag on the nearest eminence, collect some specimens for Miss Prendergast's geology class, take a snap or two, decide that the earth looks the living image of the globe in the dear old Upper Fourth, step back into the giant machine and re-set the fins, and they are home in time for cocoa, ginger biscuits and the Archers.

All very well, but the thing that I miss in space stories is drama. There is never the smallest chance that Brenda and Beryl will have a furious squabble in mid-space, pull each other's plaits, pinch each other black and blue, drill lethal holes in each other's moon suits, or try to abandon each other upon some distant planet. As they zoom along at 30,000 m.p.h., it would be stimulating to find one accusing the other of cheating at halma, of sucking up to Miss Proudfoot, of taking more than her fair share of vitamin globules.

It is clear that in future self-respecting schools will have to make an addition to their prospectuses: 'Well-equipped stables are provided, and an extensive rocket-launching pad adjoins the playing-fields. Girls are encouraged to visit Mars, but must be back in time for roll-call at 9 p.m.'

In addition to these newer attractions, the ideal school of fiction has other and older points that it must observe. It must at all costs be near the sea, preferably standing at the top of precipitous cliffs. The cliffs can either be fallen down, climbed up, or stuck on halfway. Stuck on halfway is best, for the agonizing wait enables Thirza to find the old smugglers' cave and the underground passage and to come bursting back through a secret door right into Miss Pritchard's bathroom at a moment when Miss Pritchard is least expecting her.

> Came the whine of rusty hinges, the creak of ancient woodwork, and an odour of musty, forgotten things. Smoothly a portion of

Girls will be Girls

the linen-fold panelling slid gently sideways to reveal a dusty, towsled head.

Then: 'It's me,' said a small voice.

Miss Pritchard gasped. 'Good gracious, Thirza, how you startled me,' and her dripping loofah fell back with a splash into the foaming suds.

The school grounds must contain a disused well, down which one of the new girls falls, a tidal river down which one of the new girls is swept away, and a potting shed, inside which the school smart set gives sherbet parties. Within the school there must be a boot-hole, for it is here that a really wicked girl can smoke an occasional cigarette, or put a dab of forbidden powder on her nose or a smear of *Nuit de Penzance* behind her ears.

It is essential, too, that the fire arrangements should be of the flimsiest and most makeshift kind. It is no sort of fun at all if, when the stairs are found to be blazing, Mademoiselle can make an easy way down. No: after screeching from her window in a glorious mixture of imperfect English and troubled French, she must then clamber on to the windowsill and take a spirited header into a laurel bush, emerging with nothing worse than assorted bruises and one or two simple fractures. It is the least we expect of her. Incidentally, how badly in fiction is the *entente cordiale* preserved. Poor Mademoiselle! Her French-speaking table in the dining-room is a riot of second-rate behaviour and dexterously aimed bread-pellets. The stairs outside her bedroom are relentlessly buttered and she comes purler after purler. White mice rush squeaking from any desk that she happens to open, and she cannot go within fifty yards of the cricket-field without receiving a wristy full-toss on a spot where she would least have wished to receive it. Her life is spent uttering a string of '*Mon Dieu! Qu'est-ce que c'est que ça? Ah non! Zeees is intolérable!*', surrounded by a positive Sherwood Forest of exclamation marks.

I am happy to tell you that the presence of ponies and spaceships has not made a ha'porth of difference to Headmistresses. They are still in command of every situation, prowling about upon their stout brogues and sensibly encased in tweed costumes of severe cut. Their hair is iron grey and has never known the expensive attentions of a perm. They still turn up at

Girls will be Girls

the very worst moment, just when greedy little Mona is half-way through the larder window with the major part of next day's lunch tucked temporarily into her bloomer-elastic. They still give forth telling sentences such as 'Blanche Merridew, that was a deliberate sneak. Leave the cricketing field instantly. A cold supper will be brought to you in your cubicle and I shall telephone your father after the nine o'clock news.'

I have left till last the most important ingredient in stories for girls—Rivalry. If Muriel makes a hit at the school concert with her organ solo, pulling out every stop and thundering away on the Great until the bellows rattle, then Millicent must grasp her 'cello and scrape and twang her way to even louder applause. If Muriel, panting like a grampus, wins the 100-yard backstroke in the swimming-bath, then Millicent must seize up the discus and send a record throw whizzing into the chemy lab. or, preferably, Mademoiselle. If Muriel gets ninety-eight per cent for some complicated cube roots, then Millicent must score ninety-nine per cent for her poem in the style of Ella Wheeler Wilcox. It is, and must remain, diamond cut diamond until the very last page, when the two rivals can shake hands, give each other toothy smiles, and troop off to the grubber to seal their newly found friendship amid the heady haze of fizzy lemonade bubbles.

I have one regret. It is doubtless printing expenses that now largely deny us full-page colour illustrations of situations in the text. These used to be quite splendid, and a very few words underneath were enough to explain to the less nimble witted what was happening above. I have refreshed my memory with a few illustrations from the past. There is one labelled 'Run For It' which shows two girls scrabbling through the thickest imaginable hedge, pursued by an enormous purple bull travelling, apparently, at the speed of sound. Another called 'You've Only Yourself To Blame For This, Ethel', depicts an enraged and pince-nezed Headmistress snipping off Ethel Henderson's cherished hat-ribbon in the school colours, maroon, primrose and gamboge. The text informs us that Ethel has been cheating at geography. Another picture shows Prudence Luard, arms and legs in all directions, being knocked down by a very primitive steam-roller, the explanatory caption just reading

Girls will be Girls

'Ouch!'. 'The Winning Hit' speaks for itself, and reveals Zoë Gosling making a gigantic sweep to leg with the pavy clock pointing at three minutes to six. But, alas, the ball seems to have landed tamely in a bed of stinging nettles, and there is no sign of Mademoiselle.

A FORM OF FLATTERY

1954

CERTAIN examinations in English Literature contain passages of prose and verse to which the appalled examinee must assign author and date (how fatally easy it was to be just two centuries out). Gifted readers, resting happily on their laurels, may care, just once more, to face this grim test. They are unlikely to have encountered this particular pen in any previous brush with an examiner.

> The bell was almost on the point of ringing, when Miss Whitlock chanced to look through the window. What she saw there brought her out into the playground.
> 'Girls!' she said. 'You mustn't use a tennis racket for rounders! The ball might be hit over the wall and do some damage. Understand that rackets are only to be used on the tennis-courts.'
> The group of flushed juniors, interrupted in their game, murmured an obedient 'Yes, Miss Whitlock.'
> The headmistress looked sharply at Rachel, who held the racket.
> 'You understand, too?'
> 'Yes, Miss Whitlock!'

There is no mistaking it, really. Miss Angela Brazil, at the height of her great powers. The book is *At School With Rachel*, and this particular chapter is called A Difficult Term.

Devotees of schoolgirl stories will have spotted at once that the passage comes from the well-defined second phase of a fictional schoolgirl life, the phase when spots and disasters surge up on every page and Coventry is only just round the corner. To those unaware of these three phases, it might be helpful to describe the *servitudes et grandeurs* in each of them. In fairness to Miss Brazil, it should be mentioned that the further excerpts here are from a lesser pen.

Girls will be Girls

The first phase occupies roughly the first term. Beryl may blub her heart out in her cubie in the Puce Dormy on the first night, but Lorna Hargreaves dishes her out a handful of caramels and there is always Matron, with a hearty word of cheer and an inspiriting dose to set the pulses racing. Furthermore, the first term invariably gives Beryl a chance to catch the public eye. And it is seldom a paltry triumph such as the winning of her lax colours or the rescue of a watery Mademoiselle from *la piscine*, but what one might call big stuff. Spies, perhaps.

> So this was the explanation of the flashing lights from the Station Hotel, the naval code-book in Bertha von Bümlein's games-locker, and the grim grey craft glimpsed through Miss Hope's bejewelled opera-glasses. Beryl held her breath and crept ever closer to the ugly-looking group of souwestered figures.
>
> Twixt breakers and foreshore lay a thin strip of sand over which Beryl's Kumfistroll plimsolls made but little sound as she edged her way cautiously between dead mollusc and odoriferous sea-wrack. And then, on a sudden, there came a muffled curse and an oath.
>
> 'Donner und Blitzen!'
>
> Foreigners! Sinking gingerly down onto a cushion of bulbous sea-bladder, Beryl's auburn brows puckered in the attempt to work out the language that had been used. Though only a beginner in French, she was fairly sure it wasn't that. But what, then? Portuguese? Dutch? Some little-known Dorset dialect, perchance?

Increasingly these days is the new girl's triumph concerned with horses. In comparison with a piece of devil-may-care bravery connected with these ubiquitous steeds, the beating out, unaided, of the flames that are licking their way into Miss Hopcroft's snuggery is a humdrum affair indeed. For literary purposes, the best horses are those who have had just about as much as they can take of dressage and suddenly decide to hook it over the fields to Bournemouth with maximum despatch. But they don't, poor things, ever get there.

> With a snort and an angry jangling of bridle, bit and noseband, the huge chestnut roan reared for the last time and then, sweating profusely, was still. For a moment, ashen-faced

A Form of Flattery

monitor and trembling junior faced each other across those gleaming quarters, before the former swung herself lithely from her mount. Straightening her rumpled jodhpurs, she stood gazing down at the torn gym-tunic, the towsled curls, and the slight slip of girlhood that was Beryl Frensham.

'Thanks, youngster,' said Rhoda, and try as she might to prevent it, her deep contralto held the semblance of a wobble. 'That was . . . pretty plucky of you. No bones broken, I hope, eh?'

Beryl attempted to speak but the pain from her bruised sternum changed her words into a groan. Then, with a little choking gasp, she threw up her arms and measured her length on the sun-dappled turf.

Phase two is, as stated, less happy. Fifteen is hardly a fortunate age for either sex, and poor Beryl is in constant hot water. There are showers of order-marks from Mademoiselle, impots from Miss Battersby ('I must remember where I am' one hundred times) and a series of shattering rows with her friends. These dramatic sets-to are vitally important and there is frequently one per chapter.

A horrified silence fell in the Ketelby Room as a white-faced Beryl Frensham laid down her violin and advanced slowly across the polished parquet to where Eileen Parsons was completing a run of faultlessly executed glissandos. The metronome ticked on but its relentless beat went unnoticed. Then, with arms akimbo, Beryl spoke.

'How dare you steal my resin?'

Eileen, sensing danger, stuck the prong of her beloved Lamorna 'cello even further into the floor and eased herself hastily into a more defensive position.

'But you're mistaken,' she fenced, 'I have my . . .' She got no further. At the sight of Eileen's confident gaze, something seemed to snap inside Beryl. To a general gasp of dismay, she lunged forward and thrust her shoe defiantly into the major bulk of Eileen's cherished instrument. Her taunting cry of 'There!' was nearly drowned by the splintering of varnished woodwork and the deep booming protest of the bass string.

This sort of unsatisfactory episode understandably plays Old Harry with Beryl's nerves. She is late for Fire Drill (Mademoiselle, in a fawn peignoir, takes roll-call), muffs her elocution exam with some side-splitting Spoonerisms, and her geography goes all to pieces. This last shortcoming involves her in a scene with the headmistress.

> Miss Riley narrowed her eyes and the tear-drenched Beryl wondered what could be coming now. How long had she been sitting here? Ten minutes? Ten years!
> 'On the honours board behind you,' continued Miss Riley, 'I observe the name of your mother. It is one of the few names picked out in gold, for she was, and is, among the staunchest of our Old Cholmondeleyites. As you see, she was in her year Victrix Ludorum, Monitress responsible for posture and gymnastics, and the winner of the coveted Bryce-Parkinson award for The Girl Who Has Done Most. In addition . . .'
> The measured tones ground on. Beryl's lips trembled anew and a burning tear coursed down her cheek and splashed onto Miss Riley's cherrywood escritoire.

This line of attack may be thought to be unfair, but when a girl is simply not pulling her weight there are, so to speak, no holds barred.

And now to phase three and the eighteen-year-olds. Here grandeur is indeed the order of the day. Beryl has come safely through the ruck and is now installed in the Prefects' Room ('Drag up a pouffe and help yourself to a Digestive'), with cocoa parties up to all hours, an eye to the juniors ('That new kid, Laura Lumley, was showing pretty good form at the nets') and some heartening confabs with Miss Riley about that trouble in the Magenta Dormy ('Frankly, Miss Riley, Elspeth Parker and Blodwen Hume-Davies must *go!*'). In this phase, tone is all important, and with it, culture ('Beryl had hung her Picasso above the fireplace, and now, humming the slow movement from Futti's *Spumantimento*, she was wondering what on earth to do with her Watteau'). Our final excerpt shows Beryl and a chum taking full advantage of their present status.

> Arm in arm, and sporting the lime-green and maroon blazer which was the special thrill of every passing youngster, Beryl and Muriel strolled contentedly in the sunshine.
> 'Hi! Cut that out, you two,' curtly ordered the former to two startled juniors who had been desperately trying to force their way into the raspberry canes. 'And didn't I dollop you both

A Form of Flattery

out a second go of lentil shape at luncheon?' she queried. Two alarmed heads nodded. 'Then, as a punishment, you can go and get my tea ready. Oh, and,' she added with a twinkle, 'help yourself to a marzipan slice at the same time.'

'Thanks ever so, Beryl,' chorused the juniors as they sped on their mission.

The two chums lounged on. Just one more week at the dear old school. And after that? For Muriel there was an opening in her mother's kennels at Feltham, but Beryl was as yet undecided. But whatever it was, would anything ever be as lovely as this last term had been?

There is a short answer to that question. No.

BEST-SELLERS OF THE CENTURY

1958

(a) *The Rosary* by Florence L. Barclay

FOR SHE'S A JOLLY GOOD FELLOW

FLORENCE L. BARCLAY'S *The Rosary*, published simultaneously in England and America in 1909, brought to its bulkier feminine readers a cheering message of hope for the fuller figure, the sweet, plain face, the heart of gold with the solid but concealed charms. It brings it, no doubt, still.

The heroine, the Hon. Jane Champion, is not pretty. Her coils of brown hair are skewered with 'well-directed hair-pins' and she is thirty years old. She is of almost massive proportions and nobody has yet 'apprehended the wonder of her as a woman'. She is an excellent golfer (doing the seventh in three, if you please) and goes in for tailor-mades, starched linen collar and cuffs, a silk tie, and a soft felt hat with black quills in it. You'll want to know her weight. Twelve stone-odd.

We glimpse her first at Overdene (the Duchess of Meldrum's place, you know) in an atmosphere that smacks strongly of *The Young Visiters*, with footmen in mulberry and silver livery, gold spoons for the ices, and tea under the cedar ('Muffins, crumpets, cakes and every kind of sandwich supplemented the dainty little rolled slices of white and brown bread-and-butter.'). Enjoying the crumpets, though it is high summer, is a house-party of delightful girls and handsome men, among them the rich and colourful artist, Garth Dalmain, aged twenty-seven, with brown eyes, sleek black hair, a pale-violet shirt, a dark-violet tie, and red silk socks for evening wear.

That night there is to be a concert for the county; local talent to begin with and then the great Madame Velma is to sing 'The Rosary' (music by Ethelbert Nevin). 'She will sing only one song at the concert; but she is sure to break forth later on and give us plenty.' But Madame Velma doesn't break so much forth as down with a throat ailment. What is to be done? Jane, fresh from the links, volunteers to substitute. Raised eyebrows all round, until Jane confesses that she has been having singing lessons from Madame Marchesi in Paris and from Madame Blanche ('Stop! Ah, *vous Anglais!*') in London. She confesses more:

> 'Music means so much to me. It is a sort of holy of holies in the tabernacle of one's inner being. And it is not easy to lift the veil.'
> 'The veil will be lifted tonight,' said Myra Ingleby.
> 'Yes,' agreed Jane, smiling a little ruefully, 'I suppose it will.'
> 'And we shall pass in,' said Garth Dalmain.

For the purposes of singing, Jane slips into something loose (soft black dress, old lace at the bosom, single string of pearls). Seated at the Bechstein, before a packed concert-room, she begins:

> The hours I spent with thee, dear heart,
> Are as a string of pearls to me;
> I count them over, ev'ry one apart,
>   My rosary, my rosary.

She has a deep, rich voice, 'low and vibrant, as the softest tone of 'cello. . . . This was not a song, this was the throbbing of a heart.' The audience is enthralled (cries of ' 'core'), and the effect on Garth is electrifying (hitherto Jane has been 'old chap' to him). The blood drains from his face, his eyes shine like, apparently, burning stars, and he imperiously thrusts the spent contralto back on to the platform to repeat her triumph. Burning stars give way to 'a light of adoration'.

> For a moment he did not speak. Then in a low voice, vibrant with emotion: 'My God!' he said, 'Oh, my God!'
> 'Hush,' said Jane; 'I never like to hear that name spoken lightly, Dal.'

Girls will be Girls

Garth then kisses each of Jane's largish brown palms 'with an indescribably tender reverence'. Jane is inclined to banter: 'Here you go, almost turning my steady old head by your rapture,' and she prosaically enters up her diary at bedtime: 'Sang "The Rosary" at Aunt 'Gina's concert in place of Velma, failed (laryngitis)'. But out in the deer park, communing with the stars, Garth is beside himself: 'I have found her, the ideal woman, the crown of womanhood, the perfect mate for the spirit, soul and body of the man who can win her. . . . Ah, grand, noble heart.'

Grand, noble hearts were dearer to Mrs. Barclay than likelihood. She made her aims as a writer of fiction clear:

> Never to write a line which could introduce the taint of sin or the shadow of shame into any home. Never to draw a character which should tend to lower the ideals of those who, by means of my pen, make intimate acquaintance with a man or woman of my own creating.

Each of her books was composed, complete, in her head before she wrote a line. 'She let it rest', her husband tells us, 'in the chambers of memory, perhaps for years.'

The Rosary had lain resting for more than a year when Mrs. Barclay suddenly seized her writing-case in the train between London and Hertford and wrote in full the tenth chapter (it is one of the meatiest). Shortly after, laid low with a heart strained by a taxing bicycle ride, she dashed off the rest ('Her pencil flew over sheet after sheet without pause').

The tenth chapter finds the house-party assembled again, this time at Shenstone (Lady Ingleby). Jane reads the *Spectator* on the journey down and is 'soon absorbed in an article on the South African problem'. She arrives in time for the men's singles final (Garth in that violet shirt again) and sees her adorer win, if a trifle mysteriously ('The ball touched ground on Ronnie's side of the net and shot the length of the court without rising').

Out on the terrace after dinner, with Jane again in her diva's dress (the pearls have been swopped for a cluster of ramblers), Garth proposes, perhaps a little tactlessly: 'I have never had any big things in my life. . . . This need of you—this wanting you—is so huge. It dwarfs all that went before.' He kneels, clasps his arms about her, and buries his face in the old lace.

But noble Jane, gazing at herself later in a sage-green wrapper, decides that an artist *'must* have flawless loveliness' and that her face, seen day after day above the breakfast coffee-pot, will exacerbate her suitor. Next day, in church (organ-playing Garth has dismissed the blower and they are alone at the chancel steps), she tells him that she cannot marry 'a mere boy'. Why, incidentally, is the coffee-pot moment always taken as the yardstick of domestic bliss? One can think of more trying things for unacceptable faces to be seen above. Sheets, for instance.

When Messrs. Putnam's Sons agreed to publish *The Rosary*, they stipulated that Mrs. Barclay should cut out 10,000 words. 'To do this,' Mr. Barclay reveals, 'was somewhat of a trial to her. . . . One literary friend, not knowing the circumstances, pointed out to her that one or two parts needed some lightening. . . . It was in those parts where the blue pencil had ruthlessly cut out some amusing scene.' In 1923, the complete edition (from which we are quoting) appeared, with the amusing scenes restored, and a comparison with an earlier edition could tell one which they are. There is certainly a lot of simple fun with the Duchess's talking macaw ('Now then, old girl!'), and even golfing Jane has her lighter moments:

> 'What did you go round in, Miss Champion?' inquired one of the men.
> 'My ordinary clothes,' replied Jane.

Garth, rebuffed and deeply hurt, retires to his 'lovely home' at Castle Gleneesh. Jane, now tipping the scales at eleven stone ten, spends two years in foreign travel. Some may think that, in her description of her heroine being pulled and pushed to the top of the Great Pyramid ('She had done it in record time'), Mrs. Barclay really goes too far. The four exhausted Arab guides are, however, delighted with Jane in her Norfolk coat and skirt of brown tweed (plenty of useful pockets). 'Nice gentleman-lady! Give good backsheesh, and not sit down halfway and say: "No top!" But real lady-gentleman.'

Girls will be Girls

In Egypt, Jane hears that Garth has been blinded in a shooting mishap, 'potting bunnies'. Naturally, Garth was not potting them himself, but courageously expostulating with those who were. No character of Mrs. Barclay's would willingly shoot anything, though one does not hear of them being noticeably vegetarian at meal-times. Jane decides that she must go to him but, of course, incognito until he can find it in his heart to forgive her.

The unusual plot now requires her to rig up as Nurse Rosemary Gray and attend on the patient at Gleneesh (the similarity of voice is explained away and she never touches him, except with the edge of a saucer). Garth pours out his soul to Nurse Rosemary and after innumerable pages of delicious anguish and torture, so near and yet so far, Jane thinks it safe to reveal her identity. There is only one way to do it. She steals to the Bechstein, and once more 'The hours I spent with thee, dear heart' booms out. The blind man blunders excitedly towards her and they entwine on the music-stool:

> 'You?' he said. '*You?* You – all the time . . .?'
> 'Yes; I, all the time; all the time near him in his loneliness and pain . . . Yes, it *is* I. Oh, my beloved, are you not quite sure? Who else could hold you thus?'

Who, indeed? The wedding night is full of music—an anthem on the moonlit terrace from Garth ('Beautiful, Garthie!'), a repeat performance of *The Rosary* by Jane, and a duet of Hymn 157 as the two lovers disappear together into the house.

The stirring, wholesome story sold over a million copies and still lives on. Only last year it appeared again, considerably simplified and abridged, as a New Method Supplementary Reader, Stage 5. The classes have been levelled up (Lady Jane) and down (Lady Meldrum), and the illustrator has been more than kind to the future Mrs. Dalmain.

BEST-SELLERS OF THE CENTURY

1958

(b) *Tell England* by Ernest Raymond

THE VARNISHED TRUTH

An agreeable fireside game for literary adults is to choose the fictional school that each would most have liked to attend (state your reasons and draw a map). All right-thinking women would, of course, plump for Brackenfield College, Whitecliffe (the scene of Angela Brazil's *A Patriotic Schoolgirl*, with that charmingly breezy Miss Duckworth); and for a man, thrusting aside such delightful fancies as Llanabba Castle and Mallowhurst (where Young Woodley enjoyed the varied curriculum), one could hardly do better than to put oneself instantly down for Kensingtowe, behind whose red-brick wall and iron railings the first half of Ernest Raymond's *Tell England* takes place (the author was educated at St. Paul's).

Absenting oneself momentarily and without permission from the demanding warp and woof of classroom and playing-field seems to have presented as few difficulties at Kensingtowe as elsewhere and, in the heart of London, would be more quickly rewarding than in, say, remotest Northamptonshire. Not that Rupert Ray and Edgar Doe wished often to be up and away, as their physical and emotional needs were being fully catered for within the grounds: too fully, some might think (*The Times Literary Supplement* spoke of 'a languorous phrase or two that makes us restive').

Advertised as 'A Great Romance of Glorious Youth. In Two Episodes: School and the War', *Tell England*, an unusually mature first novel, was published in February, 1922, at a time when war-weary readers were said to be still unready for stories of those catastrophic years. They were, however, ready for *Tell England* and for the varnished truth that it provided (the book was reprinted fourteen times in 1922 alone). It is the story, told in the first person by the romantic Rupert Ray (prologue by Padre Monty), of himself and Doe, 'twins' in that they share a birthday, from their adolescent years until Ray is killed on the Western Front in the closing days of the war.

The school years, with their echoes of *Stalky and Co*, no less than *Eric, or Little by Little*, make merry reading. In the late twenties and the thirties it became fashionable for youngish writers to turn and rend the schools that had nurtured them. In tortured sentences they explained how tedious was the O.T.C., how trying the footer, how dreary the staff. Occasionally there were moments of excitement and light—a sonnet in the school magazine, perhaps, or one's gouache of the sanatorium specially commended by Mr. Tunstall: but by and large the authors had all seen something nasty in the boot-hole and were not going to forget it.

No trace of sourness creeps into Rupert Ray's account, though one could have easily forgiven him a mild outburst on the subject of corporal punishment. This is excessive and takes quaint forms. He is beaten on the knuckles by Mr. Radley for passing notes, and caned, in the same morning, for tampering with the classroom clock. His house-master gives him ten strokes in class for alleged impudence, the headmaster smacks him in the face and then beats him for breaking bounds, and here comes Mr. Radley again, lashing out with a cane at Rupert's left palm (the other one has to be protected so that he can write out a thousand lines of Cicero) to discourage rebelliousness. Tears and a pep-talk follow this last chastisement, Mr. Radley absent-mindedly holding the damaged hand the while. Shortly after, Doe is beaten up by the prefects and reduced to a semi-conscious state. But one feels less sympathy for the exhibitionist Doe. Manhandling doesn't come amiss to him. 'Do you know, I really think I like Radley better than anyone else in the world. I simply loved being whacked by him.'

Doe and Ray (yes, there's a joke about it) are born worshippers and Mr. Radley is the first of their many heroes. He is none other than S. T. Radley, the finest bat in the Middlesex team, assistant house-master at Bramhall House, over six feet tall, with a powerful frame, square chin and grey eyes. No wonder that the fatherless and sentimental boys are in constant competition for his admiration and approval. Even his moral jaws (here on the subject of cheating in Mr. Fillet's Roman History class) are pleasantly remindful of sunny days at Lord's:

> The universal habit of 'stepping back' is exactly parallel to that of arguing with conscience. The habit grows; one's wicket always falls after a few straight balls; and one's batting goes from bad to worse. Never mind, you stood up splendidly to the first two straight balls and scored boundaries off both.

It is perhaps fortunate for their moral welfare that Ray and Doe are both such promising little cricketers (strange how persons highly charged emotionally tend to shine at the crease. Whoever heard of a scrum-half blubbing into his pillow?).

And so the years go by. There are tiffs and jealousies and reconciliations (only a hair's breadth from the mawkish), cricket matches won on the very stroke of time, gay jokes from the waggish Archie Pennybet, the dreadful geniality of the school doctor, Ray's aesthetic awakening (outside the swimming-bath), Doe's preoccupation with the older, sinister, lanky Freedham (son of a Presbyterian homeopath, who has fits, 'uncanny' eyes, and encourages drug-taking in what appears to be the Baron's Court area), the ragging of Herr Reinhardt (Modern Languages), and the final triumphs—the Horace Prize for Doe, and for Ray the bitter-sweet joy of bowling out S. T. Radley in the masters' match.

The news of the ultimatum to Germany reaches Ray during a summer holiday mixed doubles:

> 'How frightfully thrilling!' said one girl.
> 'How awful!' whispered the other.
> 'How ripping!' corrected I. 'Crash on with the game. Your service. Love – fifteen.'

And ripping it all continues to be, with commissions for himself and Doe and a jovial father-substitute to admire in the Colonel:

> 'You've timed your lives wonderfully, my boys. To be eighteen in 1914 is to be the best thing in England . . . Your birth and breeding were given you that you might officer England's youth in this hour. And now you enter upon your inheritance.'

Girls will be Girls

There follows a pi-jaw in the best Radley manner ('Take a pride in your bodies . . . I expect you—you grasp my meaning'), which sound advice is quickly disregarded. The subsequent shortcomings, gloomily phrased ('the things of night': 'the strange streets': 'the shameful doorway', etc.), at least serve to reassure those of us who might have been fearing that the rather special emotional climate of Kensingtowe would take a year or two to dissipate.

But such lapses are forgotten in the preparations for Gallipoli and with the stir and enthusiasm on board the Rangoon, the 'kindly old brigadier' singing 'For *they* are jolly good fellows' to the subalterns, the funny japes of the bemonocled Major Hardy, the news of the landing at Suvla Bay, and, above all, with the meeting with Padre Monty, the book moves rapidly on to its climax—the heroic death of Edgar Doe leading an attack at Helles.

Padre Monty is, as can be seen, a bustling extrovert:

> 'I say, Doe, we're a race to rejoice in. Look at those officers. Aren't they a bonny crowd? The horrible pink Huns, with their round heads, cropped hair, and large necks, may have officers better versed in the drill-book. But no army in the world is officered by such a lot of fresh sportsmen as ours.'

The Padre, who is swiftly calling Doe 'Gazelle', is an ardent Anglo-Catholic. There is a daily Mass in the rigged-up smoking-room and a rota of subaltern servers. Doe, Ray and Monty spend part of the hot Mediterranean nights in a deserted section of the boat-deck, talking about what they choose to call the 'Big Things'. After some hesitation and shyness have been overcome, the triumphant Padre extracts promises from Ray and Doe that they will come to Confession (preparing himself for this ordeal the wretched Ray covers nine sheets of paper with past misdemeanours). Monty is beside himself:

> 'Now and then one is allowed a joy that would outweigh years of disappointment. You two pups have given me one of those joys tonight. It's my task to make this voyage your Vigil; and a perfect Vigil. It's all inexpressibly dear to me. I'm going to send you down the gangway when you go ashore to this crusade – properly absolved by your Church. I'm going to send you into the fight – *white*.'

Best-sellers of the Century

'Are we downhearted? NO', the soldiers repeatedly cried to each other. Nor, I suspect, were the 1922 readers downhearted. In the post-war years of bitterness and disillusion, *Tell England* provided an exhilarating pick-me-up. The glorification of youth, the high moral tone, the ingenuousness, the knightly theme, the bravery and self-denial of the youthful fighters—perhaps, after all, they had gone happily to their deaths and the great sacrifice had all been worth while.

> Tell England, ye who pass this monument,
> We died for her, and here we rest content.

But 1958 is another matter and the second half of this memorable book makes strange, sad reading in this day and age.

AN IMPORTANT FIND

1970

Professor J. de B. Hambrill, of University College, London, has now completed his preliminary survey of the Hartwycke papers, the extraordinarily interesting *cache* of documents discovered two years ago by a National Trust representative in a walled-up tiring room at Holdingham Hall, Suffolk. The papers, mostly in a fine state of preservation, relate mainly to the Lady Eleanor Hartwycke who, with her husband Gervase, was in her day a considerable traveller and had the wise habit of keeping 'fayre copies' of most of her correspondence, together with all her bills, both 'payed' and 'unpayed'. It is this diligence that has at last enabled light to be thrown on the great enigma of the Hartwycke fortunes. At one moment in history we find the family virtually destitute, and then a few days later astonishingly affluent and starting on the vast building programme that is one of the glories of Suffolk.

This is merely one of a string of such fortunate discoveries. It may be remembered that some years ago and under the title *Dead Letters*, Maurice Baring published details of comparable 'finds', but he only did so after proper consideration and when a respectful time-lag had ensured that there would be no possibility of causing any distress to surviving relatives of the main participants (Julius Caesar, Sir Walter Raleigh, Clytemnestra, etc.). Professor Hambrill is, naturally, reluctant at this early stage to release, before proper evaluation and then only with the permission of the Hartwycke family, the main bulk of this treasure-trove. There are, however, two letters that should be of considerable interest to historians and others and which need be no longer withheld. Neither letter can yet be dated with complete accuracy.

An Important Find

Bury St Edmunds,
Thursday.

Dearest Queen Gertrude,

What a heavenly week-end! The time just flew and Gervase and I hated having to dash down to the docks before the theatricals began but, as it was, we only just caught our packet.

How to *begin* to thank you for all the treats? That breathtaking tour of the ramparts, the fencing display, cordials in your closet, sweet little Ophelia's impromptu cabaret, and *dear* old Polonius! His puns and jokes and conundra were a delight — such a *fun* person!

It's too exciting about Hamlet's unofficial engagement (no, no, *not one word*, I promise). What a blessing that in these sadly sophisticated days he has chosen somebody as unaffected and simple as Ophelia. We adored seeing her wildflower collection and her well-stocked herbarium. Such clever little green fingers! I think you are well advised to postpone her swimming lessons until after she is safely married. A snuffly cold at the altar creates an unfortunate effect on that Day of Days.

As to the armoured apparition that appeared in our room on the stroke of midnight and started jabbering nineteen to the dozen about some orchard picnic party that had gone wrong (and who, this weather, can hope to stop flummery curdling?), I think your explanation must be the right one. It was a nightmare caused by indigestion — *no* reflection, dearest Gertie, on your tasty *smörgasbord*! At all events, we hardly heard what he said, being entirely occupied with trying to puzzle out how he had managed to come straight in through the wall. Gervase *thinks* he remembers what was said but I have told him he is wrong. Quite quite wrong.

Greetings to Claudius — how lovely to see you both already such a *team* — and thank you, thank you, thank you.

Ever your devoted
Eleanor

P.S. We leave shortly for Inverness for a week's shooting with the Macbeths, *not* our favourite couple but it seems, from a rumour we heard, that we may coincide with King Duncan's visit (just the one night, I understand), which should be quite entertaining. Actually, Macbeth, left to himself, is more or less all right, but *she* is the trouble, taking offence at the merest trifle and looking absolute daggers. We always lock our door there. Things are very apt to go bump in the night.

P.P.S. I do repeat, my dear, that we did not see or hear what at the time we thought we saw and heard. No we didn't. In these lean days (since our return it's been just bills, bills, bills) there is nothing more precious, almost, than a true friend.

The delicate hints about money were unsuccessful. With Queen Gertrude (not the world's brightest lady, and kept in the dark anyhow, and too drowsy with sex to be over-percipient) the pfennig did not drop, but very shortly after the Inverness trip the Hartwycke fortunes enormously improved, the great west wing was built, and Eleanor's expenditure that autumn on wimples alone points to an entirely stable financial position. The explanation of this is now quite clear.

Bury St Edmunds
Friday.

Dear Lady Macbeth,

You won't want to be bothered with a long letter – you'll have had so much tidying up to do – and anyway since our return I've had my hands full with Gervase and his maladies (his eyesight, chiefly). Also, we found the house in a sad state of disrepair and down here in the south (the journey took us, incidentally, ten days, but a messenger riding *really* fast, could do it in seven) the price both of labour and building materials has shot up appallingly. We have anyhow to be so careful with our pennies and as it was we couldn't afford to tip either that darling old night porter or your bonnie wee Maggie nearly as generously as we should have liked.

It was an immense joy to see you (and the grouse!) again, and just in case you should have noticed us wandering about in the night and have started wondering whether we were worried about something, I had better explain about Gervase. He suffers from an affliction just as distressing as failing eyesight and, that last night and for a purpose with which I am only too familiar, he had to leave our chamber in the wee sma' hours (I lit the rushlight and helped him out into the corridor, reminding him to turn sharp right after the lobby). Our doctor can't (or *won't*) find any remedy and, knowing that we sometimes go abroad for our holidays, makes feeble jokes about being incontinent on the continent – very French and tasteless. When Gervase returned

An Important Find

he was as white as a sheet and inclined to shiver and snuggle up to me in a manner which we have long since abandoned.

Next morning, Maggie brought up our breakfast as usual (ummmm! your *baps!*), told us the very unexpected news about the King's death (a *real* test for a hostess and you came through it *superbly*), and then the moment Maggie had gone, out it all came! I shall not even *begin* to tell you what Gervase thought he saw in the passage. Not one word of it shall ever pass *my* lips! He didn't see either of you, truly he didn't, and if he did you were both quite EMPTY-HANDED. And if you *weren't* completely empty-handed, we think you must have been helping to clear away after that *delicious* dinner.

I need hardly say that the moment we got back here I rushed Gervase off to the oculist who, strangely enough, found NOTHING WRONG!!! So it must be something else and now I'm hunting about for a really competent brain specialist but of course they charge the earth and, with lunacy being such a very unpopular disease, they threaten one with exposure (what the Froggies call *chauntage* – I believe the English word is blackmayle) and one just has to BUY THEIR SILENCE. Have you ever been subjected to this monstrous kind of extortion? I gather it's a complete waste of time trying to get away with under-payment in the first instance as the other 'person' involved only keeps coming back for more.

How I envy you the excitements of the coronation, *whoever* it may be! What are you going to *wear*?

Your true friend
Eleanor

P.S. Since writing the above, we have been twice more to the oculist (the *fees* for all this!) and he has now got rather ratty and says that Gervase has the eyesight of a boy of sixteen. Would he were similarly juvenile elsewhere!

P.P.S. Malcolm and Donalbain (the latter all the way from Ireland) are coming here for a Young Things Dance on the 24th, just three weeks from now. What a lot we shall have to discuss! Such cheerful, chatty youngsters!

CHRISTMAS REVIEWS OF BOOKS FOR GIRLS

1935

Fifty-two Sports Stories for Girls. Edited by R. S. Lyons (Hutchinson).
The Lower School Leader. By Veronica Marlow (Oxford University Press).
The Head Girl at Wynford. By Winifred Darch (Oxford University Press).
Nancy in the Sixth. By Dorita Fairlie Bruce (Oxford University Press).

LIFE in schools for girls is clearly an exciting business. They go the pace. Lights are put out in the cubicles and one would think that the girls, exhausted by the strain of ragging Miss Bellamy, would be ready for refreshing sleep. But all that the merry madcaps seem to want is the ginger-pop hidden under Bertha's bolster and a moonlight climb over the roofs. And doubtless the readers of these stories would not have it otherwise.

In *Sports Stories for Girls* there are several gripping yarns, among the best being *Gloria's Secret, Amy's Mix-up, Doreen's Ride, Gertie's Glider,* and *The Rivals of the Racquet*. In the last named there is a splendid pen-picture of the tennis final for the Chalfont Cup (missing from its case in Big Hall) between the head-girl, Monica Warren, and Rita Frazer, who has just won a scholarship to Girton.

'Whang!'
It was the first ball of the set, and on the return it banged from Monica's racquet just inside the base line, an unplayable shot.
But Rita did not lose her head.

> She stayed back at base and let the high balls bounce. She ran in to the short ones and lobbed them back. In a word, she was all over the court, showing amazing speed and endurance.

And so to the closing moments of the match.

> The ball landed, and Rita was on it like a flash. Whizz! The next shot went like a streak – *ping!* And the next, *Ping!*

Small wonder that after all that excitement poor Monica spends the night walking in her sleep round the school, returning the lost cup to its case, watched by the Headmistress, a Miss Dacres, 'all in black marocain'.

In *The Lower School Leader*, Miss Veronica Marlow has not hesitated to make full use of realism and the scene where a stubborn junior called Margaret refuses to eat up her gristle is strangely powerful.

> 'But that's all gristle!' protested the junior, 'really it is.'
> 'Nonsense. Eat it up at once. There is nothing put before you in this school that is not entirely digestible,' snapped Miss Buckett.
> But Margaret did not move, nor did she try to eat it.
> 'If you want me to be sick, I will,' she said, defiantly, 'but it's just cruelty to animals.'
> This seemed to enrage Miss Buckett. 'Take her out, please,' she ordered; and immediately two prefects left their places and more or less dragged the junior by brute force off her chair and out of the dining-room.

Never mind. Everybody has cheered up in time for the staff lacrosse match.

> Already, filling the entire gap between the posts stood Miss Jellaby, the heavyweight music mistress. There could be no getting past Miss Jellaby unless the ball went right through her. Keenly watching the match were Miss Salt, the Oak House matron, still smelling strongly of lysol, and three of the younger mistresses just down from the 'Varsity, and out came a battery of cameras to take 'snaps' of them in their glory.

And finally comes Miss Buckett herself, clutching an umbrella 'though the sun did not look like going in'.

Girls will be Girls

The Head Girl at Wynford introduces us to a charming school; indeed, as a visiting hockey player remarks:

> 'I never come over here but I envy you,' said Myra Jarvis, the Bingston captain.
> 'Why?' asked Betty, as they walked across the middle field.
> 'Your topping grounds! Your marvellous old school!'

But in spite of the scrumptious surroundings, there are the usual tiffs.

> 'I don't know what you are talking about,' Edmee observed coldly, and turned away.
> Petronel looked after her. 'Pig!' she said, under her breath.

Miss Dorita Fairlie Bruce in *Nancy in the Sixth* excels in her choice of names. There are Desdemona Blackett, Geraldine Judkins, Ryllis Rutherford and Clemency Walton. The heroine, Nancy Caird, who is a ripping bat, is unable to get to the all-important match against the Lady Foresters.

> Seated on the bank beside the useless bicycle, Nancy fumbled in the tool-bag, and one or two involuntary tears splashed in upon spanner and screwdriver before she was able to get to work on the flabby tyre.

Nancy is ambitious to win the Woodford-Leigh Organ Scholarship, but there are difficulties.

> 'That's what I thought!' burst out the organ-master explosively, 'but I didn't want to make any ill-founded accusations. When I asked Mrs Paterson as a very special favour to allow you to use her organ, I gave her an undertaking – a solemn undertaking – that neither of you would do it any damage. I told her that you could be trusted – you were not beginners; I practically pledged my honour that no harm would come to her instrument – and what has happened? This morning I get this note from her to say that she could hardly get through the morning service yesterday because some of her most important stops were completely out of action!'

Christmas Reviews of Books for Girls: 1935 and 1936

Three of the above books bear the noble imprint of the Oxford University Press. Oh well, *il faut*, no doubt, *vivre*.

CHRISTMAS REVIEWS OF BOOKS FOR GIRLS

1936

Prefects at Springdale. By Dorita Fairlie Bruce (Oxford University Press).
A Schoolgirl in Switzerland. By Kathlyn Rhodes (Harrap).
The Winifred Darch Omnibus. Containing: *For the Honour of the House; Cicely Bassett, Patrol Leader; Margaret Plays the Game* (Oxford University Press).

Gusto streams from these packed pages and one reads breathlessly on and on.
In *Prefects at Springdale* there is a bizarre recluse called Miss Peters who enlivens her conversation with cries of 'Hoots toots' and 'Tits, lassies!' She offers a prize for the most go-ahead house. The girls are in a great flutter. What shall they do to be go-ahead?

> 'This idea at least,' said their house-captain triumphantly, 'is entirely my own. It came to me – just came to me – in a blinding flash. Girls, this house is going all out for domestic science.'

And they do too, eventually winning Miss Peters' prize, which turns out to be 'a pot of exquisite Eastern workmanship, containing a dwarf cedar tree, gnarled into a perfect miniature'. The names of the girls who receive this charming trophy are Marion Banister, Louise Sturges, Isolt Kingsley, Tibbie Macfie and Fearnelith Macpherson.
The girls are all fearfully keen on a ripping games mistress called Miss Stewart, and can one wonder? 'It isn't her beauty and her auburn colouring, but she's got that—that sort of

glamour.' She abandons lacrosse momentarily in order to go for walks with a plucky little junior called Faith Kersey, who has 'eyes liked drowned violets' and is an 'undeveloped genius at throwing-in'. It is Faith who canoes down the flooded main street to the rescue of two girls who are singing hymns while imprisoned in a ruined tomb. Meanwhile, the plot requires the headmistress, a Miss Timmins, to try to shin up an extremely high wall. Need I add that she reaches the top?

A Schoolgirl in Switzerland is a riot of violent wiggings from the headmistress and stern punishments. Lucia, who has a Sicilian great-grandmother, is to dance the Tarantella at an hotel for charity, but she takes the wrong shoe-bag. Elma hurries after her with the correct one, gets caught in a storm, loses her purse and receives a tremendous reprimand, partly in French. Then Elma goes back for her Kodak, misses the bus at the St. Bernard Hospice and is told to write out 'I must remember to wind my watch' a hundred times in French and English. Then Rosalie smacks Elma's face for having ruined her water-colour sketch when attacked by a savage goat and, refusing to apologise, is shut up in the sanatorium. Then Lucia is set upon by a lunatic in the Castle of Chillon and, soon after, Rosalie steals Gwen's flute and hides it in Elma's work-bag. Gwen is incensed ('She flung herself on Elma and snatched away the flute, recklessly pulling stitches out of Elma's beautifully knitted sweater'). And even in the holidays, Elma is found in a casino, heavily made up, and Lucia is seen dashing about on the beach in a bathing dress called La Sirène.

In *Margaret Plays the Game* the girls are extremely fond of theatricals and of the English mistress, Miss Rylands. Margaret, who lives in a house called Red Clamps, is a splendid little actress, who does not hesitate to let herself go.

> 'You were *it*, Margaret,' murmured Thetis Standen. 'I should have wept in another minute. But if you're going on being so intense all through the play, you'll be a rag at the end.'

Rosamund, a girl with 'red-gold plaits and dazzlingly fair skin' is head prefect, an unjustified appointment to some.

'Rosie carries being "all things to all men" a bit far. I often wonder what she'll do in a really tight place where pretty ways and book-cleverness would cut no ice.'

Quite so. Rosie can't even see that Doris Gilmour has heels more than three inches high.

'And though the Head was too old-fashioned to suspect the presence of powder, teint Rachel, not only on her nose, Doris had boasted that on Saturdays she used lipstick as well.'

LITERARY PITFALLS

(a) IT WAS A NIGHT FOR LOVERS...

1967

THE reason why I no longer read romantic novels is that I find in them a repetitive quality which doesn't exactly lift the heart. Ever a glutton for the printed word, I have in the last fifty years ploughed through a vast number of novels, even after I had passed through the young and hopeful stage of expecting each new one to be another *Decline and Fall*, another *Esther Waters*, another *Bleak House*. I have found increasingly that the same well-worn and somewhat old-fashioned sections of fictional life appear as regularly and as predictably as the moon, and indeed are very often about the moon and the emotional burblings of entwined couples as they gaze soulfully up at it.

> It was a night for lovers. 'We've a right to live, Blodwen,' and Rodney caught her to him. 'We can't fight this . . . this magic. But, my dear, what have I said? You're trembling.' And for answer, and with a little sob, Blodwen gave him her lips.

In this country we don't yet go in for those knock-out opening sentences at which American writers excel. You know the sort of thing.

> 'I was gabbing with Lefty on the corner of Madison and 44th when up comes this guy with a gun.'

But we do have our own English way of getting the thing fairly smartly off the ground.

> 'Heavens but you're beautiful!'
> The sallow-faced stranger half hissed, half breathed the words as through heavy lids he feasted his smouldering eyes yet again on the loveliness that was Gloria Passmore. And indeed

Literary Pitfalls

> the tribute was not undeserved. The Hunt Ball at Passmore Hall was at its height and Gloria, in an audacious gown of mauve velours with generous *décolletage*, made an arresting picture. The famous Passmore emeralds gleamed at her throat, her bosom rose and fell to the lilt of a lively Eric Coates, her nostrils quivered with the sheer joy of being alive. Gloria was, that night, all woman.

Yes, yes. Fine work, apart from the physical difficulty of half hissing, half breathing even a simple request for a glass of water. It is quite lovely to think of Gloria being all woman. But I have a literal mind. What, may one ask, had she been at 10.30 that morning? A little of each? We can only hope that her husband, Sir Jasper, has remained male throughout the 24 hours. We don't want malicious chatter in the village. It is some reassurance to realize that the charwoman, a Mrs. Kindlysides, has undoubtedly been all day all charwoman. Incidentally, this kind of tale is often called *Tomorrow is Yesterday*, or *Yesterday is Tomorrow*, both statements being inaccurate.

In a page or two the Hunt Ball is over, the guests have gone, and the sallow stranger has insulted Gloria.

> 'What was that he had called her?' she mused.
> 'A painted bore?' Something or other. She had barely listened.

Sir Jasper, full of port and peevishness, has retired for the night. Gloria, alone at last, wanders out on to the terrace to cool her temples. 'Temples' is the novelist's polite word for indicating those portions of Gloria which have become overheated during the exertions of the final waltz and require cooling. There she is now, out on the terrace doing it. In real life, this would be the moment for an agitated servant to appear bringing woeful domestic tidings. 'Please, m'Lady, there's eighteen glasses been broken, and a plate of salmon mousse has got itself wedged inside the piano.' But this is not real life.

Now, in all Gloria's trials and tribulations there's one thing she can always rely on. The weather. It's going to match her mood. It's an as-old-as-the-hills trick used by most writers, good, medium and oh-dear. If Gloria's temperament is sunny, up zooms the thermometer into the 80s. If she's morose,

Girls will be Girls

grey skies are a certainty. And now, wounded, rejected, reviled, the elements don't let her down. The novelist gets out his all-purpose stormy weather section and lets fly.

> From the East, a scud of malodorous hill-fog was clutching, with greedy fingers, the lower slopes of High Crag, while to the South the angry black clouds massed above Spume Tor were moving to the attack like great galleons which have crowded on full sail and, feeling the wind in their bellies, now sought to fright and put to rout the flurries of hail from the North. Westwards, a sea-mist was snaking up through Shaggy Bottom and ever and anon a clap of thunder gave defiant answer to the tongues of forked lightning that played above the shuddering moorland. The rain, whipped by the storm, lashed Gloria with the violence of a sjambok, but she heeded it not.

As a weather forecast, this is on the muddling side but it's safe to say that a mackintosh would not be an indiscretion.

Before we leave the Passmores, as leave them we must for the suburbs are calling us, let me say that this novel is sure to have an Indications of Wealth section. It is the sort of thing that Buchan sometimes went in for. Sapper too. You would think there was enough—the terrace, the emeralds, the Hunt Ball, the piano, the salmon mousse—to show that Sir Jasper hasn't yet joined the bread line. But readers, it seems, never tire of opulence. It's easily enough displayed.

> 'Mornin', Sir Jasper.'
> Old Trowel put respectful finger to gnarled forehead as the bejodhpurred owner of Passmore Hall reined in his giant chestnut stallion, Sultan, and gave the wrinkled head-gardener a curt good-day. Sir Jasper was fresh from an inspection of his little world – the spreading acres of barley and hot-house, seakale and cold-house, kitchen garden and market garden, brood-mares and asparagus-beds and trout-streams and coverts and pleached limes and forced rhubarb. Just an ordinary corner of old England. But his corner. His.

As for Old Trowel, he has been thinning out the nectarines. Soon he'll thin out the peaches. Then he'll sweep out the small orangery. Heigh-ho. Just another humdrum day.

And now to a novel usually called something like *A Lady*

Literary Pitfalls

Went A-Begging or, more pretentiously, *Come Dance For Me, Mildred Faraday*. It is specially intended for middle-aged married ladies living, perhaps, in the London Commuters' Belt. *In* things, and yet somehow out of them, with dull-seeming husbands and children at school and . . . well . . . what *is* there to do? Satan has an answer (and that's a possible title, too).

> 'Not bad for forty!'
> Mildred Faraday gave an amused chuckle as, seated on the embroidered Regency pouffe at her walnut dressing-table, she flung the words triumphantly at the serene woman facing her in the oval barbola-work mirror. With another contented little laugh, she passed smooth hands over the muscles of her neck and shoulders and then, springing quickly up, she threw back, on a sudden impulse, her flimsy black lace négligée. 'Not bad!' she said again. And again, 'Not bad!'

All woman once more, I'm afraid. Mildred is for ever doing things 'on a sudden impulse' and the purpose of this one is to give the reader an eyeful of her charms. For what Mildred really means by 'not bad' is 'not good'. She is about to make an ass of herself with Barry Carstairs, recently met across a crowded room and ten years younger. Her husband is conveniently away on a Continental business trip. Indeed, his postcard—a coloured view of the main railway-station at Hanover—lies before her, and reads 'Have secured the Grundwerk-Windleben order for 1,800 flange-pins. Good-oh! Returning Monday. Cheers. Hubert'. Dear, prosaic old Hubert.

And at this point in the story, the writer shows himself to be but human. Novelists lead strange lives, lives comparable with those of factory workers before the affluent, golden age in which, so we are told, we now live. Novelists are underrewarded and over-worked. They rise soon after dawn and, if their fumbling, chilblained hands will allow, they brew a cup of Instant Hey Presto coffee before, at 8 a.m., settling to their grisly task. At midday, with 2,000 words and a splitting headache behind them, they knock off for a breather. From eleven o'clock onwards they've been feeling pretty peckish and it's strange how their thoughts of food communicate themselves to their fictional creations. Nobody looks very attractive while

Girls will be Girls

munching and it can only be the writer's own hunger that now prompts Mildred to ask Barry to take her out to dinner. She suggests the Ristorante Stoggi in Greek Street. This outing gives the novelist a chance to go into his intimate dinner routine, with exuberant foreign waiter.

'Do you come here often?'

Barry voiced the query as, with the slightest of pressures on the sleeve of Mildred's skunk opera coatee, he guided her beneath the welcoming neon sign. She vouchsafed no reply, merely indicating the beaming waiter who came hurrying forward. 'Ah, Meees Mildred, it is a long time, yes, no, but Gaston, 'e do not forget. Your favourite corner table? *Voilà*. And a vase of nasturtiums? So. *Un plaisir, ma'mselle.*'

Gaston then switches on a number of pink shaded lights and alerts the staff with loud finger-clicking and cries of 'Philippe! *Vite!* Hercule! *Voyons! Allons donc, mes petits! Avanti!*'

Mildred, relaxed and at ease with herself, bestowed on Gaston one of her swift, fleeting smiles. 'Now, *mon ami*,' she bantered, 'we're going to put ourselves entirely in your hands.' She sensed that Barry was innocent of the ways of Soho and she gloried in being able to surprise him. Gaston leapt to the challenge. 'You 'ave ze 'unger, *n'est-ce pas? Bien!* Let me see now . . . I suggest a dozen Whitstables, zen potage Gaston, suivi de 'ow-you-say whitebait, a roast bird, and an *omelette flambée* which Gaston will flamber for you 'imself. And to drink? A Saint Bernard 1966 well chilled. *Tout de suite.*'

Mildred is only very slightly suspicious when she finds herself paying the bill (£14 5s. 9d.) and lending Barry his taxi-fare home. Next day she goes into the cocktail cabinet routine and the opening love sequence. Barry, invited for 6 p.m., compliments her on her cocktail-dress and she says 'Thank you, kind sir' and drops him a mock curtsey. Then, while pouring out her second dryish martini, she suddenly stops dead and starts to beat her head on the illuminated cocktail cabinet.

'Oh Barry, Barry my darling, what does it all mean? I'm so tired of everything . . . tired, tired, tired. My life with Hubert . . . it's just a foolish sham. Something has died inside him.'

Literary Pitfalls

There was a hint of desperation in her voice that her strained look and the pulsing of her temples did nothing to belie. Striving to calm herself, she plunged a wooden cocktail stick into a maraschino cherry and forced herself to eat.

But Mildred is wrong. She has under-rated Hubert. She hasn't paused to think what Hubert might be doing that weekend before 'returning Monday'. After all, novels are read by men as well as women and Hubert too is having a fling. Stationed in Germany at the end of the war with the 187th NAAFI Canteen Repair Company, flaxen-haired little Gretchen had nursed him back to health and strength after a tea-urn had fallen heavily on his right foot. The acquaintance had ripened. Gretchen had winning ways and a light hand with *Apfelstrudel*. Her *Vater* kept the local *Bierhaus* and Gretchen was the life and soul of the bar-parlour, with a *Prosit* here and a *Gesundheit* there. In the summer months her mother let her stay out as late as 9.15. And now here is Hubert trying to find her again, and successfully. There she is, flaxen plaits all in position, still dishing out the watery lager. There is a lot of 'Is it? Can it be? *Mutti*, look who is here! It is the Lieutenant Faraday! *Du lieber Himmel!*' There are sentences such as 'Across the years, their love called to each other. She had been kind, had the little Gretchen!' Gretchen can now stay out until 9.40. Prosaic old Hubert indeed!

There now! I fancy I've provided you with your very own do-it-yourself fiction kit. Start now and construct your own personalized romantic novel. But please don't ask me to read it.

LITERARY PITFALLS

(b) I FIRST SAW THE LIGHT OF DAY . . .

1967

It is said that we could each of us, if we wished, write one novel, and it is clear that, for obvious reasons, we could all write one autobiography. Just put the words down and there you are. The great thing is not to. The unwholesome urge to spill the beans must be fought. It is to me an urge as mysterious as that which sends climbers up unscaled north faces, or which causes a man, gazing at himself in the looking glass, to decide that the ideal moment has arrived for sporting a moustache. I do not understand these strange promptings. We all first saw the light of day somewhere, but let us, so to speak, keep it dark. This path is strewn with quagmires.

Ancestors are always perilous material.

> The Pogsley family hailed originally, I believe, from Northumberland. Indeed, parish registers show that there have been Pogsleys at Chitterton since the Great Plague.

Plague indeed! The pages now erupt in a nasty rash of Pogsleys and their assorted corruptions, the Pigsleys, the Pegsleys and the Pagsleys, until, around 1890, and with our heads in a whirl, we come to a game old bird called Gramps Pogsley, a sturdy widow living in reduced circumstances in a bleak part of Yorkshire.

> Everybody in Sodhurst respected old Gramps as she pottered about the small village store whence came her modest livelihood, busy, aye, but never too busy to deny a neighbour her wise counsel or to bestow on a kiddie one of her cheery smiles.

Gramps's staunch behaviour frequently inspires some dreadful literary inversions, such as 'Good she was and brave she was and kind she was to us children'. Gramps is, however, highly skippable (hop speedily to the next page). Skippable too is the slightly dotty relation signalled by some such sentence as 'My Aunt Felicity was something of an eccentric'. We know full well what will follow: Aunt Felicity's tricycle, her talking parrot, her elaborate and ornate hats in which birds have attempted to build their nests. And there are her jokes. Heavens, her jokes and her *bons mots*, which now sit so solidly on the page and qualify as *mauvais mots*. The truth is that if you don't have a father like the Sitwell one, relations are best not mentioned at any length unless they are definitely unusual. If they have committed murders or changed their sex, you could just

Literary Pitfalls

mention it briefly in passing, but mum, in this connection only, is generally the word.

Many male autobiographers appear to have been misunderstood at school. There is, however, a sharp difference between scholastic sufferings before and after the first World War. The pre-1914 victims usually took it all on the chin.

> At Fairfields College we had our own version of football, a game called Bladder, at which I was the completest duffer. Many a promising passing movement came to grief when the ball, or *puff*, reached my trembling chilblained hands. Screams of execration would greet my feeble attempts to carry the *puff* over the *bummage* and score a *dowsel*. Later, in the big dormy, my punishment was swift and certain. A row of scowling praepostors, armed with the traditional bludgeons – black woollen stockings filled with tintacks – lashed mercilessly out at me as I dragged my weary body to the noisome ablutionaries. They were but doing their duty. I richly deserved their belabouring. Indeed, it helped to make me what I am today.

Which of course implies that what the writer is today is pretty good.

The style of that excerpt tells us that it was somewhere in the early nineteen-hundreds, a period particularly rich in theatrical and operatic memoirs. A warning here about chapters called 'An Amusing Mishap'.

> During the 1906 season at La Scala there was an incident at which I still guffaw. The celebrated tenor, Emilio Spotti, was singing the great role of Costivo in Buffa's *La Disgrazia*. Emilio was at that time of generous *embonpoint* and, being somewhat lacking in inches, usually sang from some sort of platform. He had just come to the famous aria in praise of Sunny Italy, *Che Grande Macaroni*, when we were appalled to see a dangerous wobble in his podium.

And so on, in a shower of chuckles, to the phrase which goes, 'and how we got to the end of the act I shall never know.'

The post-1914 schoolboy is, alas, a more fragile bloom, and in this kind of autobiography there is often a wronged, whining note which does not exactly move one's hard heart. Sometimes these sections are in diary form.

Girls will be Girls

14 *July* 1926. My resignation from the O.T.C. has been ill received by the petty little Kitcheners who run it. It's caused a stir and it was meant to. The officers are as common as they are silly. Major Bulstrode, he of the purple face and bad breath, exploded over me in the Armoury in a rainfall of spittle. 'Wretched little pacifist,' etc. etc. As an additional defiance I've joined the Scouts.

Later went for a stroll with Adrian to Chugley Wood but there was a thunderstorm. During prep, got on with my novel, *The Strange Metamorphosis of Simon Quest*. Chapter one's going pretty well.

16 *July* 1926. Matron found my sonnet to Adrian in my handkerchief drawer and gave it to Willoughby who read it out after prayers as an example, if you please, of bad writing. I fumed all evening. Next day during bathing was able to hide behind Pringle and push Willoughby, fully clothed, into Splosher. Pringle was swished after roll-call. Have given up writing and espoused palette and brush, but Mr Oliphant says my ink and colour wash of Adrian lacks both form and power. What does *he* know? If he could paint himself, he wouldn't be here trying to teach us.

And so on and so forth, in mounting resentment, until the long-suffering headmaster decides that the school has, perhaps, no more to offer him.

I am always amazed at the powers of memory of most autobiographers. Old men may forget, but some old men remember far, far too much. There is one thing I have noticed in the passages which concern their time as undergraduates at Oxbridge—the many dull and undistinguished friends they must willy-nilly have made have apparently been wiped from their minds. They have dropped totally away and only the real dazzlers remain.

My closest chums at Trinity were 'Stuffy' Bretherton, 'Tiny' Markham and 'Pips' Jellaby. With them I laughed and fought and romped my way to that First in mathematics on which my heart was set. Never were there better fellows. We were literally inseparable. Woe betide a host rash enough to invite one of us without the others. A ducking in the college fountain served to reveal to him the enormity of his sin. Small wonder that envious wags dubbed us 'The Four Musketeers'.

Literary Pitfalls

By now a constellation of asterisks has appeared and, peering down at the footnotes, we find heart-lifting news.

> 'Stuffy' Bretherton, a future Lord Chief Justice. 'Tiny' Markham, later the first Viscount Bognor. 'Pips' Jellaby, now Professor Sir Julian Jellaby, O.M.

So much glittering success palls quickly. One longs for somebody, a much more humble friend, called, possibly, Eustace Calfsfoot, to redress the balance by being a total failure at everything, his modest career also enshrined in a footnote.

> Poor Eustace came to nothing. His commercial venture in Maida Vale foundered, likewise the place of refreshment which he and his spirited wife, Thirza, ran at Gravesend. In the evening of his days he has however contrived a little niche for himself as night watchman at a disused zinc-mine in, I believe, North Venezuela. They also serve who only sit and watch.

And so to the autobiographer's closing years, the away-from-the-rat-race section with the rustic life calling—if what he eventually finds can be called rustic.

> For some time we had been a-weary of London life and the increasing calls upon our time and energies. Many an afternoon did we spend tramping the lanes of Hertfordshire in the hopes of finding that dream home which we felt was somewhere there, beckoning to us. And it was thus that, late one September evening with the light just beginning to wane, we stumbled on Groynes.

Have you noticed that country 'places' possess, more often than not, weird monosyllabic names—Groynes, Twytche, Flankes? Something tells me that somewhere, in Derbyshire perhaps, there is a vast antique pile called, quite simply, Belch. The great thing to do with a country place is to alter it completely. Here is the lady of the establishment at work.

> At Groynes, Mona was in her element. With her green fingers she created from its seven acres of garden a veritable

Girls will be Girls

paradise. She put the formal beds down to grass and chopped down the yew hedges as being harbourers of the slugs on which she had waged war. We threw out a new and modern wing and pulled down the stables. 'Vandalism,' hissed our neighbours, but we did not care. Yes, at Groynes, and at last, we were happy . . . happy . . .

There is included a picture of Groynes, a rather lop-sided building in the middle of a jungle. In the foreground stands a formidable lady, with trug and secateurs, browbeating a cringing gardener. Underneath it says: 'Mona discussing exciting future plans with Diggit'.

It takes a great man *not* to write a lengthy autobiography. John Buchan, for instance. 'I cannot believe', he says in *Memory-hold-the-Door*, 'that the external incidents of my life are important enough to be worth chronicling in detail.' Remember that, please, as you recall that amusing picnic with the Pogsleys at Paignton in 1912 and start removing the cover of your typewriter.

CHRISTMAS REVIEWS OF BOOKS FOR GIRLS

1937

MEMSAHIBS IN THE MAKING

Dimsie Intervenes. By Dorita Fairlie Bruce (Oxford University Press).
The Dorita Fairlie Bruce Omnibus. Containing: *Nancy at St. Bride's, That Boarding-School Girl, The New Girl and Nancy* (Oxford University Press).
Elinor in the Fifth. By Winifred Darch (Oxford University Press).
Audrey on Approval. By May Wynne (Ward Lock).
Growing Up at St. Monica's. By Jessie McAlpine (Oxford University Press).
Gillian the Dauntless. By Frederica Bennett (Nelson).

WHAT is up with the Girls of England? This year's batch of stories contains far too many references to beauty culture. Are Hilda's plaits as glossy as Thelma's? Where is Patience's bejewelled hair-slide? Who has tampered with Eileen's cold cream? This is unhealthy stuff, and let this be the last of it.

In *Dimsie Intervenes*, the Headmistress has a hard time of it: 'My dear, I am never off duty except when I'm in bed—and not always then.' Some of the girls are keen on their appearances and purchase bath-cubes, freesia soap and bottles of Anti-Freckle from Boot's. To counteract these, there are the Anti-Soppists who troop down to the gym, anxious to practise 'those last leg movements of Miss Mallory's'. The Seniors have a percussion band in the basement and the climax of the story finds Dolly Ansell being laced into a pair of stays in the lower music-room, where 'many dark deeds had taken place'.

In *Nancy at St. Bride's* there are Helga Grub ('a slim dainty-looking Senior'), Betty Muffet ('wispish-looking') and Charlotte Truscott, the head girl, who has 'exchanged the big glasses of her younger days for a trim pair of pince-nez'. The dormitories are named after fruits—Gooseberries, Apricots, Nectarines, etc. Sybil 'takes up' Nancy, and even Christine, 'yellow hair' and all, is 'drawn to her', but Nancy will have none of it: 'I think you're a perfect pig, Christine Maclean! The horridest Senior in the whole school!' Nancy is very wild and if she isn't upsetting herself in a canoe or getting cigarettes from the pier, she is in trouble over her 'topsy-turvy drawers' or up at the 'skreigh of dawn' and painting a skull and cross bones on the school boat. And even before the story begins there have been troubles. One of the characters muses about the school's past history and utters the most remarkable sentence that I have ever found. 'It was the summer of the great gale when the san. crashed into the sea—stirring times.'

In *Elinor in the Fifth* there are some topping mistresses: Miss Vance, busily occupied with her cyclostyle, the gym mistress who does 'caterpillar crawl down the empty lower corridor to relieve her feelings' and favours a stiffish brew of tea, Miss Brown ('young, round and rosy') and the Head herself 'in the severely cut coat and skirt that she wore during all but the hottest weather'. There is a tremendous row between Elinor and Rosemary: 'She even called me all sorts of things and banged the Lab. door in my face.' And there is one unpopular mistress, Miss Ellis, who really gives the girls what for: 'Nobody would think you had just come from a gymnastic lesson. Look at your sitting postures now! Disgraceful!'

Audrey Trevorne of *Audrey on Approval* has a mother who 'is obviously a sport', the Trevorne eyes ('dare-devil blue') and an uncle who is a rich recluse. She visits him in Cornwall and comes in for a lot of Cornish dialect, bats (referred to as 'airymice'), and a dear old Cornish soul called Mrs. Wherry, from the fishing world ('It's the prattiest sight to see t'mack'rel brought ben').

Audrey's uncle is overcome by fumes from fluids which 'have drenched the linoleum in his laboratory', but Audrey is thoroughly on the spot:

A towel lay beside a basin of water; she soaked it and flung it dripping round her head. The water trickled down her face and into her eyes, but she did not care.

And goodness me, how Miss May Wynne can write when given half a chance:

> Who minded a scramble when sun-kissed wavelets were dancing over the golden sands. Evening mists were rising over the moors, drawing a mysterious curtain as though pulled by fairy hands, hiding the secrets of the Little People who love the heather and moonshine.
>
> Those dear, dear moors! How *could* she leave them?

How indeed.

In *Growing Up at St. Monica's*, the girls have 'a keen desire to know more about Nature' and there are some fascinating open-air botany lessons with Miss Telford:

> 'Ah, I see a sand-martin up by those rabbit-warrens.' Miss Telford put her field-glasses up to her eyes and focused them on a grassy knoll. 'And look, there is a puffin. Come, Agnes. Come, Vera. We mustn't lose sight of this elusive bird.'

In class too, Miss Telford never lets things lag:

> 'An order mark for both of you,' said Miss Telford grimly. 'Hang the map on the board, Kathleen. Marjorie, name the British colonies in Africa. Attention, everyone. Sit up straight.'

In a book rich in incident and characters we have Miss Denton, a wealthy neighbour, who is robbed of her 'dear old Russian leather handbag', Vera Winter, the school bowler, who is constantly 'loosening up her arm-muscles', and Meg Elliot, who practises Bach fugues on the boot-room piano and announces 'a common or garden spot forming on the side of my nose'. And Miss Jessie McAlpine can be thoughtful too:

> Some people would laugh if you asked them to play a game of cricket by themselves, yet they think nothing of playing the game of life single-handed.

In *Gillian the Dauntless* we meet a highly-strung Russian girl called Mystica Degris, given to 'long shuddering sighs that shook the girl from head to foot'. She is steeped in mystery, captured by Bolshevists in Paris and has eyes that make one think of 'vast forests with pathways strewn with countless years of pine needles'. She appears in four pictures—being tripped up by wire, examining a padlocked parrot's cage, peering nervously from a window, and being knocked down by a motor-car, in colours.

Girls, shie away your bath-cubes and freesia soap. A moonlight night and a rope ladder were all your mothers ever needed to make them happy. And give those stays to Mademoiselle.

CHRISTMAS REVIEWS OF BOOKS FOR GIRLS

1939

FROM SANTA'S WORKSHOP

The Term of Many Adventures. By May Wynne (Nelson).
The Rector's Second Daughter. By Kathleen Conyngham Greene (Harrap).
The St. Berga Swimming Pool. By Theodora W. Wilson (Nelson).
The Jolly Book for Girls (Nelson).

The Führer's reckless *démarche* occurred too late in the year to enable our gallant authoresses to prepare for this Christmas such heartening yarns as *Madcap Monica of the Maginot Line* or *Vivandière Vera.* So this year the girls' books are the usual gay round of scrumptious study teas with that spiffing Senior, Hyacinth Duggleby, rags in the cubies (and no quarter with the bolsters) and diamond cut diamond on the lacrosse field.

The Term of Many Adventures is well named. Mrs. Hinford, who has moved her school to an ancient Jacobean house and brought 'her thirty lassies out into the wilds to develop', knows a thing or two: 'Too easily assumed responsibility is hurtful

Christmas Reviews of Books for Girls: 1937 and 1939

both to rulers and ruled. It creates that masterful spirit which we see bringing chaos in adult life.' Quite so. So she abolishes prefects and deals ruthlessly with any hanky-panky ('she trusted her girls and expelled them if they failed her'). On the staff there is a bogus widow called Mrs. Lysden 'whose husband is at present a convict in Dartmoor Jail' and after a successful literature class she thanks her pupils with 'Girls, you have been sports'. She has a son called Barry, 'such a friendly little chap' who is partial to 'a lubly brekkus wif an egg and storberry jam'. Prominent among the girls is Mogs Gordon ('as jolly and sporty as any boy') who will 'be a topping nurse for wounded soldiers when she's grown up—do you know what I mean?' It is she who rescues little Barry from the gypsies in a chapter called 'Mogs of the Loyal Heart'. There is also a mysterious Indian who refers to the girls as 'The Missie-Babas' and looks 'as though he might be a Thug,' and a Mrs. Mingleton 'who made a very great point about being her boys' "big comrade" and "elder sister Mum".'

The Rector's Second Daughter is Nan Hawker, who has 'charm in her freckled face, in her smile, which showed one little crooked tooth, in the dimple at the corner of her chin' and should you be tempted to doubt it you can see her picture on the cover depicting Nan fresh, apparently, from the most demanding room in a Turkish bath and wearing an arresting blouse covered in mauve stripes.

The St. Berga Swimming Pool begins dramatically with Pat receiving from her dying mother ('hot stuff in mixed tennis for years') advice on how to win the tournament: 'Grip—grip that racket. Never go flabby and slack.' So it was 'a quiversome moment' when Pat reached the school centre court, but 'she played all out to ramp through' and by dint of 'scooting in the right direction at the right moment' trounced a muscular strongly built girl named Maud Graham 'whose speciality was the 'cello'. In the end of term concert, Joan Chesterfield distinguishes herself by singing in *Night and Day*, 'a simple cantata which seems to have turned into an operetta'. Lady Chesterfield, Joan's grandmother, is not keen on her taking up singing and wants to keep her 'in prison in the Kensington flat', until the Vicar gives her a good talking-to, referring

Girls will be Girls

sombrely to 'The Prince of Fear'. Then Joan sings 'Come unto Me' at the Sunday concert and, as a novel encore, confesses to a cardinal misdemeanour and rushes from the room, the awkward pause being tided over by Miss Jordan ('Come Maud! We will have your 'cello solo'). Lady Chesterfield is a Daisy Ashford character who lives in Bellevue Mansions and 'indulges in very choice China tea at nine o'clock with cake which she has sent from Edinburgh.' She goes to a concert, faints and is carried out. She is recognized by the audience: 'That was Lady Chesterfield!'—that was.

The Jolly Book For Girls is very very jolly indeed and includes a gripping tale called *Fire!* by Betty Ferguson. Eileen and Cora are in the laboratory, experimenting with nitrogen, but Cora is nervous: 'Don't be so panicky, Cora,' retorted Eileen tartly, and a moment later, of course, she is a mass of flames and being rescued by the Headmistress. Then 'nasty little stories went round, hinting that Cora had deliberately allowed Eileen to burn.' However, when the stables catch on fire, it is Cora who frees the horses, lies 'burbling unintelligibly' in the San, and eventually emerges from Coventry surrounded by roses addressed 'To the Bravest Funk'.

CRITIC'S CORNER: LADIES

CONFINED JOY

We Danced All Night. By Barbara Cartland (Hutchinson, 1971).

1920! On with the dance, let joy be unconfined and in the centre of it, with her 'restless, twinkling feet', twirled honey-packed Barbara Cartland, since those days a tireless purveyor of romance (over 90 novels notched up, among them *Love Holds The Cards* and *Love Is Contraband*) and now a gleaming telly-figure with a niagara of jabber and the white and creamy look of an animated meringue, here harking back down Memory's Echoing Corridor to the Twenties, a bright old person come to put us right about the bright young people.

This indigestible feast of period gossip, launched with maximum publicity, kicks off with a proposal of marriage ('This was living! This was life!') at salubrious yachtsville Bembridge, and quite soon a 'jolly major' gets into a muddle with his revolver ('The bullet whizzed through my hair with a deafening report.') Never mind: 'Men wanted me. I had forty-nine proposals before I finally said "yes".' Every girl tried to look like Gladys Cooper:

> I was a pale imitation of such loveliness, but still of the same mould. Fair hair fluffed over the ears, large rather surprised eyes – mine were actually green – red lips.

It was a small world in which 'everybody' danced, either to a cranked-up portable or at the swish Embassy Club, a world dotted with the smart modish nicknames of Circe, Poppy, Bibs, Toto, Buffles, Fruity, Baba, Cupid and Pingo. Nobody thought it at all odd when Santos Casani demonstrated the Charleston on the roof of a taxi bowling down Regent Street. Anything went. There were Treasure Hunts all over London ('Cries of Tally-Ho!') and Servants' Balls at Harrod's.

Girls will be Girls

Bewitching (it seems) Miss Cartland was placed upon a pedestal. 'The young men treated me as if I were made of Dresden china.' They did more:

> Men who loved me would stand outside my house late at night, on the evenings I did not go out with them, in a silent salute . . . They would write me poems, and there would be flowers. 'Good morning, darling,' one note read, 'I want these roses to see you.'

An unexpected delight for the Gloire de Dijon, *n'est-ce pas?*

There was so much to be *done*. From Bembridge one shot over to Deauville for a chat with the Dolly Sisters and King Alfonso, leafed through the *Bystander* for mentions, smoked ('Have a gasper'), jigged up and down on a pogo-stick, helped out with the Princess Royal's appearance ('I sent the girl who did my nails round to Lord Lascelles' house'), had wistful thoughts about life ('If you and Daddy had a divorce, you could marry another Daddy and Daddy could marry another Mummy'), took part in country house japes, lent a hand with the general strike ('Lady Diana Cooper had been sitting up all night to help fold *The Times*'), joined a killing follow-my-leader through Selfridges, and answered invitations to baby parties:

> We are having romps from ten o'clock to bedtime. Do write and say you'll come and we'd love to see Nanny too. Pram-park provided.

Cocktails were served in nursery mugs, dummies were sucked, and screams resounded up and down Rutland Gate till all hours.

Miss Cartland's pages are chock-a-block with tumbril talk and why there wasn't a revolution one will never know:

> Millicent Sutherland was naturally beautiful, but she also took 'trouble' with herself. When she was over eighty she always made up her eyelashes, rouged and powdered her face, and arranged her well-waved hair before she allowed anyone to see her. How can the girls today, with their greasy uncombed rat-tails, sunburnt and neglected skins, fingers stained with nicotine, compete with that?

Millicent Sutherland was 'of course' a rich and leisured Duchess long since dead. It is no fault of hers that she should here be resurrected to give point to Miss Cartland's ungenerous, complacent and displeasingly self-assured views. If honey is indeed what makes her tick, I'm sticking to the chunky Oxford. And hand me my knitting.

AT A PINCH

A Wiser Woman? By Christabel Aberconway (Hutchinson, 1966).

Lady Aberconway's merry recollections are varied indeed. Oscar Wilde peered into her pram. Mrs. Baldwin, keen on straight bats, organized cricket matches for her ('I was good at fielding'). There were chats with Shaw ('a brilliant old boy') and Wells (she had to insist on a vertical friendship) and Sir George Sitwell ('Is there much incest in this part of the world?'). And in and out of the social swirl pop the tireless Ladies Cunard, Colefax and Lavery. The charming authoress has been widely loved and admired. We even find Dr. A. L. Rowse weighing in with a letter beginning *'Chère Déesse et Pédante'*. *Déesse*, certainly. Her (modestly described) beauty brought out, alas, the beast in men. At a tender age, an amorous and unfragrant tramp attempted a familiarity with her ('I remember that my mother gave me an aspirin'). Shuffling, with Osbert Sitwell, late into a theatre, 'I was given a fearful pinch on my left buttock. It was a most savage pinch.' The culprit? Lord Alfred Douglas. Then a porter at Calais selected the same plump portion for a manly nip, and later on Thomas Hardy forgot himself before luncheon: 'He gave me a surprisingly strong, virile pinch, again on my left buttock: all three pinches have been on that side: I wonder why?' Of the three pinches, recollected in tranquillity, Lord Alfred's comes out as the sharpest. Blood will tell.

Parties sometimes brought a gay misunderstanding:

> Clive Bell, plump, with long reddish hair swirling round his head, was sitting on a high chair. Beloved Augustus John saw this figure from the back, put out a hand, feeling for the breasts,

and gently stroked the circled wreath of hair. Suddenly he saw his mistake and quickly left the party.

It is all as harmless and sweet as candyfloss but if Lady Aberconway is going in for racy talk, either she or her publishers must get it right. How on earth do gentlemen 'pump-shit'?

I SPY

The Murder of Mata Hari. By Sam Waagenaar (Barker, 1964).

When Mata Hari (*née* Margaretha Zelle) returned at the height of her notoriety to her native Holland, the *Nieuwe Rotterdamsche Courant* inquired dramatically, 'Priestess, dancer, lady? People ask—and guess?' We now know the answers and they are 'never, certainly not, and, alas, no'. On that occasion she mimed a series of eight 'moods', among which virginity, chastity, and fidelity were defiantly included. Though not precisely a *grande horizontale*, she did tend to get chummy rather quickly with rich gentlemen. Obesity, that built-in Dutch hazard, attacked only those parts that are better plump and on these a succession of wealthy industrialists sought to press their suits.

After an unhappy youth spent shunting about between relations, she married a middle-aged and diabetic Dutch colonial officer improbably called Rudolph MacLeod. He had advertised for a wife and Margaretha had speared him out of the classified ads, prudently enclosing with her reply a recent snap. Her grasp of the truth was never firm and later on rheumaticky Rudolph became a full Colonel, then Sir Macleod, and was finally ennobled as Lord MacLeod. By then she herself was Mata Hari ('The Eye of the Day' in Malay) and, penniless in Paris in 1905, she took to dancing, or rather to gyrating slowly in a half-light and removing her clothes. She was 29 and dark and there was about her a hint of the mysterious East. She encouraged the belief that she was the daughter of a Javanese prince and that her home-made dances were sacred and oriental.

Critic's Corner: Ladies

She did not deceive Diaghilev or Colette ('she did not actually dance but with graceful movements shed her clothes'), or Lord MacLeod ('she's got flat feet'). Wherever it was possible and profitable to shed interesting items—here a veil, there a bejewelled breastplate—Mata Hari shed. We find her at La Scala, the Folies Bergère (in *La Revue en Chemise*), in Cécile Sorel's conservatory, at the *Cercle Artistique et Littéraire*, and at a cosy supper-party for four ministers of state ('she regaled them with her art'). It was the most successful strip-tease since Salome.

Her end was in keeping with her muddled and bogus existence. Arrested by lynx-eyed British officials at Falmouth in mistake for Clara Benedix, a German suspect, she was released and went to Spain. Here the French identified her with German agent H-21, for reasons wisely still unvouchsafed, and her own fatal gift of the gab did the rest. She confessed to having been approached by the German consul in Amsterdam and given a sum of money to encourage her to spy: but that was all. Even her 'secret ink' turned out to be a contraceptive fluid. Mr. Waagenaar makes out a case for her that rings very true. It was 1917 and a convenient year for a meaty French scapegoat. A last prison photograph reveals the bewildered and harmless Dutch bourgeoise that she was. She met death bravely and many would agree with her husband's verdict: 'Whatever she's done in life, she did not deserve *that*.'

SEATED ONE DAY AT MY UPRIGHT

Unfinished Symphonies. By Rosemary Brown (Souvenir Press, 1971).

There is electrifying news for music-lovers the world over. The great composers who, in our blindness, we thought dead are at it yet, thudding and thumping on their astral Steinways and kindly communicating their latest *morceaux* to a busy, Balham-based housewife, Mrs. Rosemary Brown. You scoff?

Girls will be Girls

You disbelieve? Even when there is a foreword by the Bishop of Southwark? Come, now!

Liszt turned up 'by teleportation' about 10 years ago ('I was a little shy with him at first') and, finding Mrs. Brown hard up, suggested 'with a little twinkle' a flutter on the football pools. The result? Dividends of £10 and £51 ('It may sound strange but I can quite truthfully say that I feel Liszt to be a great friend', and I should hope so too). He has also accompanied her to the supermarket and advised on the purchase of bananas, totting up the bill effortlessly (it seems that the higher regions have not yet been decimalized).

Liszt has at intervals brought along others and between them they have dictated over 400 musical compositions. Naturally, you'll want the latest news. Well, Bach is still 'not very talkative' and has lost weight. Debussy's beard has gone, he has taken up painting, wears kinky clothes and is 'somewhat mercurial' (words for his new songs are supplied by 'somebody called Lamartine'). Beethoven and Schubert first popped along in 1966 (that missing last movement is as good as in the bag). Chopin, 'apt to drop into French when excited', is all Gallic charm ('If you do not call me Frederick, I will not call you Rosemary'). Poulenc has looked in, ditto Mozart (whatever K number are we up to by now?). Einstein has dictated 'an equation' but tends to fade. Language is no difficulty, the non-English speakers having 'made the effort' to learn it 'over there'. Oh, and if you want a good chuckle, Berlioz is your man.

Of Mrs. Brown's sincerity there is no question and she has impressed many ('We wondered whether you could ask Liszt to ask Berlioz about two metronome marks in *The Trojans*'). There is certainly something pretty rum about it all. Even to take the compositions down requires considerable experience and it seems possible that Mrs. Brown's musical ability is greater than she modestly allows. But of course, on this rather absurd level, there is a flaw. There is nothing remotely agreeable about the act of musical or literary creation. In her humdrum heaven, with its Berlitz language schools and King's Road shops, are decomposed composers really condemned to go on composing for all eternity? And if so, what of other skills? Do plumbers plumb, coal-heavers heave and ironmongers

Girls will be Girls

ARTHUR MARSHALL

HAMISH HAMILTON
LONDON

*First published in Great Britain, 1974
by Hamish Hamilton Ltd
90 Great Russell Street London WC1
Copyright © 1974 by Arthur Marshall*

SBN 241 89044 6

*Printed in Great Britain
by Ebenezer Baylis & Son Limited
The Trinity Press, Worcester, and London*

monger? On these important points perhaps cheery old Liszt could flash yet another newsy bulletin to Balham.

ROLL THEM

Norma Jean. By Fred Lawrence Guiles (W. H. Allen, 1969).

Norma Jean, before Ben Lyon invented the name Marilyn Monroe for her, posed for photographs and operated in Los Angeles through the Blue Book Model Agency (*directrice,* Emmeline Snively). While emerging from girlhood, Norma Jean had taken on some surprising contours but was never a classical beauty. And what a *lot* there was to learn for somebody with too long a nose:

> 'Lower your smile,' Emmeline instructed Norma Jean. 'It's the shadow, dear. There isn't enough upper lip between the end of your nose and your mouth. Try smiling with your upper lip drawn down. *There!* Now your smile keeps your nose in place. Just practise that a while.'

When she moved on into films there was, in addition to the contours, the provocative buttock-swinging walk: 'Emmeline Snively attributed Marilyn's ambling gait to weak ankles, but Marilyn herself said that she had always walked like that.' And in addition to the walk there was the simple fact that when they loaded up the film camera and stuck Marilyn in front of it, the 'flesh impact' on the screen was comfortingly profitable.

But alas, her road to world fame (the inscrutable Japanese found her especially *troublante* and scrutable) was strewn with the mangled bodies of friends and helpers. *Life,* delighted with some appealing photographs, might call her the 'busty Bernhardt' but 'she was shaky about so many things: modern art, authors' names, acting'. She was also shaky about tolerable behaviour. She walked out on films, she was for ever late, she was humourless, and her fuzzy connection with reality was unhelped by champagne and vermouth ('her favourite insulation when fretful'). Husbands and lovers came and went, and were glad to go. Latterly, she abandoned, when fretful, vermouth for nembutal, sometimes needed 47 takes for the simplest scene and, venomous and apathetic by turns, and ungrateful, selfish and silly to the last, sank away into drugged oblivion. At her death they did not switch off the Hollywood lights for her. Indeed, many in that unfeeling world would have voted for extra illuminations.

ALL A LADY NEEDS

Norah. By Lady Docker (W. H. Allen, 1969).

In Lady Docker, Anita Loos's heroine lives again. 'All a lady needs to know is where she is going and what she demands of life.' Norah Docker, an orientated traveller if ever there was one, found her way unerringly to three millionaires (Henekeys, Cerebos and the BSA Company). 'I have never undressed in front of any of my husbands. . . . Call me prudish, call me old-fashioned, or what you will.' What you will is fine.

After kicking off as an exhibition dancer at Frascati's, her excitements began. Gentlemen became friendly ('Once, when I was being wooed by the Ninth Duke of Marlborough . . .'), pink champagne flowed and, with the firm cooperation of the French manager of the Queen's Hotel, her virginity went pop in Birmingham. And so to the first millionaire, Clement Callingham, and with him the gracious life of Maidenhead and a charming domesticity ('We were in the bathroom—Clement was in the bath and I was on the loo'). After two abortions and an attempt at Confirmation ('I will have to inform the Bishop of Reading'), motherhood was safely celebrated in a giant marquee, 'the chefs marching in with a ham on which they had designed a life-size facial picture of me in gelatine.'

After Callingham's death, she passed to the elderly Cerebos king, Sir William Collins, 'Wilkie' to friends ('His family crest bore the motto "Salt Satisfies" '), who called her 'little girl' even during those agitating weeks when he changed his will ('I clipped him angrily over the top of the head with the

New York Times'). During his illness there was another shock: 'I found one of the night nurses in bed with Wilkie . . . Wilkie, in his collapsed state, thought the nurse was me!' Oh, I *see*. There was just time to get the silly old will changed back before the sorrowing widow found herself being proposed to in a Bournemouth potting-shed by an octogenarian judge ('his inflamed daughters came to me protesting').

And on to Sir Bernard Docker ('I pursued him relentlessly'), with her young son playing his role expertly ('Do you want to marry my mummy, Uncle Bernard?'). Love's call was answered. 'Days now dawned with a tingling dew, in the field of life we walked together,' either into Claridge's or the Dorchester or the golden Daimler or into the sea-going Shemara ('Our only real home'). And, snugly housed, one could muse on one's success:

> Was the secret in my hazel eyes? Or, if I wasn't the most beautiful woman in the world then what was it I possessed? The opinions sometimes entered the realms of complexity.

Occasionally possessive Bernard got ratty ('He hurled several ornaments, including a clock, at me'), but there's almost nothing that a big box of deep mauve orchids can't put right. And now in the mellow evening of her days, courageously fighting off taxes in Jersey, Lady Docker ends her hilarious phantasmagoria on a thoughtful note:

> I have learned one bitter lesson from life. It is, that money cannot buy friendship. I never expected it would, but I thought it might, at least, induce appreciation.

This question, too, must remain in the realms of complexity.

UPS AND DOWNS

Skittles. By Henry Blyth (Hart-Davis, 1970).

'Skittles' (born Catherine Walters), the famous Liverpudlian dockside *fille de joie*, burst upon a startled Fulham in the late

Girls will be Girls

1850s, about to graduate from ordinary prostitution (one night stands) to the more respectable career of *demimondaine* (attachments of a year or so). Skittles only count when lying flat, and her many admirers included William 'Bawdy-house Bob' Windham (Old Etonian rake), Lord Hubert de Burgh (Old Harrovian rake) and Aubrey de Vere Beauclerk (Old rake). The Marquess of Hartington (Spencer 'Harty-Tarty' Cavendish) set her up in Mayfair and, becoming a dashing equestrienne, she was the cynosure of all eyes in the Park, Alfred Austin informing us disapprovingly that 'ladies in Society speculated endlessly on her doings'.

At the age of 24, she removed herself and her doings to Paris. Clever Mr. Blyth, devotedly burrowing, finds that there seems to have been an oddly virginal quality about her which luckily brought out both the beast in men and their paternal and protective instincts. She was speedily pounced upon by Achille Fould, 63 years old and, conveniently, Minister of Finance, and was naturally resented by her rivals, Cora Pearl, *née* Emma Crouch (*spécialités*: whipping, orgies and assorted novelties) of whom there is a snap in outstandingly unbecoming knickers, the nymphomaniac La Barucci (a fool for a uniform), and La Païva (whose *hôtel* is now, suitably enough, the Travellers Club). Skittles also managed an *affaire du coeur* with Wilfrid Scawen Blunt (Old Stonyhurstian), a converted Catholic who was able to overcome, for one or two *nuits de folie*, his fear of eternal damnation and who longed to be, of all things, a matador.

Back in London, Skittles raised her sights. The Kaiser waggled those moustaches at her. Napoleon III 'eyed her lustfully', and our own Prince of Wales made with the *oeillades* and, probably, something else ('Our poor Boy stands so alone, alas,' wailed inaccurately his august Mother). Gladstone ('Old Glad-eye' to streetwalkers) was appreciative and sent a birthday present (Russian tea). It was all a success story if ever there was one. She lasted on, incredibly, until 1920, taking the waters at Tunbridge Wells and gamely nursing her arthritic limbs in South Street, her death certificate describing her as 'Spinster of no occupation'. Ahem.

Critic's Corner: Ladies
THE GOSPEL TRUTH

The Vanishing Evangelist. By Lately Thomas (Heinemann, 1960).

On the afternoon of May 18, 1926, the titian-haired Aimee Semple McPherson, gifted evangelist of the Angelus Temple, Los Angeles, stepped into a warmish Pacific for a dip and, after some porpoise-like activities, disappeared from view, thus beginning one of the most sensational rumpuses of the Twenties.

A thorough search started. For days on end, frenzied Four Square Gospellers braved the surf, sailors let down grappling-irons, divers dived and aeroplanes roamed the waters, their pilots ready, should Aimee be sighted, to fly off and waggle their wings over the Temple as a signal to Mrs. Minnie Kennedy, Aimee's mother and business manager, that her daughter was no longer asleep in the deep. Guards stood by to protect the body; it was feared that determined souvenir-seekers would attempt to make off with selected portions of Aimee.

After the first shock Minnie bore up real well. The Temple continued to dispense its bizarre spiritual comforts and, when all hope seemed gone, a memorial service for the eminent divine netted a cool $34,190 in 'love offerings'. But still no body could be found. Where was Aimee when the tide went out?

She was, as it happened, some miles away. At 1 a.m. on June 23 she appeared to a startled slaughterhouse custodian on the Mexican border with the tale of a woman cruelly used. She had, she announced, been lured from the beach by kidnappers while still in bathing togs and, smartly chloroformed, had been driven away and held, bound and captive, in a desert shack. Sawing through her bonds with the aid of a jagged tin, she had escaped and had just completed a fourteen-hour trek across the broiling wastes.

Yet the fugitive showed no signs of distress or dehydration. Her dress was clean and her kidnappers had also thoughtfully supplied her with a wrist-watch and a strawberry-pink Bon Ton

Girls will be Girls

corset, just her size. Attempts to locate the shack failed as Aimee's recollection of it, apart from the fact that its sanitation was unusually watery for a desert, was vague (the shock, you know).

Amid the general rejoicings at her resurrection, doubts grew. Aimee's handsome and attractive ex-radio operator at the Temple, Kenneth Ormiston, was found to have inhabited, with a begoggled 'Miss X', a seaside love-nest at Carmel for a period exactly covering the evangelist's absence. 'Miss X' was strangely like the Temple pulpit spellbinder, who had previously known marital bliss with a 'Holy Roller' Pentecostalist and a wholesale grocery clerk.

Others had seen the uneasy pair meeting furtively in hotels and a Mrs. Oberman had noticed the living spit of Ormiston with Aimee just before her final plunge. Faced with these wounding accusations and a grand jury investigation, imperturbable Aimee continued to immerse baptismal candidates, while Minnie devotedly continued with her totting up of the day's takings.

For month after month the affair, like some inexhaustible firework, exploded on. Readers of this wildly funny account, most wittily assembled by Lately Thomas, will have their own favourite episodes. There is a jolly moment when a female jury member, examining some Carmel grocery lists allegedly in Aimee's handwriting, departed with a hasty 'excuse me' to the ladies' lavatory. She returned flustered and empty-handed and we must assume that the valuable pieces of paper evidence, which were seen no more, went floating discreetly down to the sewage-disposal plant at El Segundo.

BRACE YOURSELF

Letters to my Daughter. By Edith Summerskill (Heinemann, 1957).

Letters to my Daughter contains groups of Dr. Summerskill's letters to her daughter Shirley. At first the writer is in the

Critic's Corner: Ladies

Antipodes, the only woman on a 1944 parliamentary delegation, and no doubt the letters were welcome to her family. The effect they now make in published form is banal and dreary, what with Dada's leave-taking carnations, shampoos and sets, deck quoits, an MP dressed as a Hawaiian girl with water melons in his brassière ('Most amusing'), laddered stockings, Tasmania ('Off we flew'), and Adelaide, in 'a tastefully furnished suite. . . . As I had an hour to spare before lunch I sat on the balcony and held my tired pallid face up to the hot sun. . . . The next day was the coldest I have experienced in Australia and I donned my woollies.' And so on and so forth. Despite excitements such as the singing of 'For They Are Jolly Good Fellows' and freesia bouquets, home matters are not forgotten: 'I am sorry to hear that Happy has had another scrap. He was very plucky to take on an Airedale.' For a delirious moment, this reader thought that Happy might be a coloured servant who had gone berserk, but he turns out to be a Sealyham.

With the last groups of letters (during Oxford and hospital training) the suspicion arrives that it is not Shirley who is being addressed but us. Dr. Summerskill, megaphone up, is on the bridge and off we float on a sea of clichés with hobby-horses bobbing all around. What uncomfortable breakfasts poor Shirley must have had, gulping down statements about sex relationships, the child-parent problem, colour discrimination, the family behaviour pattern (dingy phrase), the importance of the genes in mental balance, and shattering bromides such as 'Only a woman can smile while her heart is breaking' and 'Human nature in castle and cottage is the same'. Men are selfish beasts, inclined to be disastrous in the home and not much better out of it. And as for those Impressionist painters! All this is paraded without a shred of humour and in a tone to set the teeth on edge:

> Now that you have left home – at least temporarily – I am bracing myself to withstand your cool, detached reappraisal of your family. Do not feel that this may be interpreted by us as in any sense disloyal. It is part of the process of growing up to see your family in terms of the community.

Girls will be Girls

Occasionally Dada ties up 'a rebellious rambler', and we remember a visit to *The Mikado*, but on the whole, life is real, life is earnest, and by golly, life is gloomy. *Il n'y a pas de lettres ennuyeuses*, said Dumas. Oh yes, there are.

MARVELLOUS PARTY

I Married the World. By Elsa Maxwell (Heinemann, 1955).

In *I Married the World*, the inexhaustible hostess and 'social bulldozer', Miss Elsa Maxwell, provides the most rumbustical autobiographical *mélange* in the language. There are over 300 packed pages and the Index boasts (how rightly) about 800 names, most of them what is known as household, with others (Mrs. Lydig Hoyt, Cholly Knickerbocker, Buggsy Siegel, Mrs. O. H. P. Belmont, Morton Baum) having the curious lilt that makes them likely to be American household. In the last chapter of this feast, just as one is longing for a water-ice, no fewer than eight Dukes are served up, floating in a rich sauce and with all the trimmings. Lengthy study of this odd book must make even the most party-minded reader wish for nothing more exciting than baked beans *nature* in a Hammersmith café.

Miss Maxwell certainly began as she meant to go on, being born in the public eye in a theatre box in Keokuk, Iowa, during a performance of *Mignon*. Even her nurse was unusual—an exotic male Chinese called Hi Foo, who got himself mixed up in the tong wars and was later hanged for murder. At the age of sixteen months, she won a babies' beauty competition in the Mechanics Pavilion at San Francisco, staying on long enough for the earthquake, though this disaster did not prevent her struggling through the rubble to keep a lunch appointment with Caruso. When, on a private occasion, Adelina Patti obliged with 'Comin' Thro' the Rye', the youthful Miss Maxwell sang it right back at her.

Further activities of this determined lady include being taught six-pack bezique by Winston Churchill and meeting, *chez* Mrs. Cuckoo Belleville, the Prince of Wales (a snap, at a later date, shows him looking at Miss Maxwell in a manner that can only be described as thoughtful). She had her ear playfully tweaked by Joffre, arranged a clambake on the Lido for Queen Marie of Rumania ('This is utterly delightful'), shared Princess Margaret's ham sandwiches, witnessed the opening of Cheops's grand-daughter's burial chamber with Queen Elizabeth of Belgium ('eerie'), and was among the privileged few invited to hear John Drinkwater read *Abraham Lincoln*, for which literary treat the hostess, Lady Colefax, prudently locked her guests firmly in.

The saving grace in all this bewildering rigmarole is the subject's ability to laugh at herself. She has done much good work for charity: she has wit and charm and there is something fetching about this abundant zest for life, if it be a life that most of us would fly from. She is, in general, friendlily disposed towards other junket-throwers, though there is an occasional hint of criticism of Mrs. Perle Mesta ('An invitation to one of her routs carried as much distinction as being circulated by a neighbourhood supermarket'), of Mrs. Gwen Cafritz ('The Hungarian bombshell with a wet fuse'), and of a foreign Prince ('Born with a built-in Geiger counter that led him unerringly to untapped heiresses'). There is, alas, much fatiguing jaw about whether Miss Maxwell was or was not on good terms with the Duchess of Windsor. Either way is all right.

Psycho-analysts' noses may well twitch at the information that little Elsa, not invited to Senator Fair's glittering party in his elaborate mansion across the street, sat at her window, 'too proud to cry', watching the gorgeous guests stream in: 'I swore to myself I would give parties all over the world . . . to which everyone would want to come.' She has done just that. After an especially good dinner-party, she muses:

> Why did they come? Surely it wasn't my beauty, wit or even the dinner, excellent though it was. It may sound immodest to the point of arrogance, but I honestly believe they were attracted by the gaiety I radiate as naturally as I breathe. As far back as I can remember, I've always been like a little girl on Christmas morning. I wake up every day with the unshakable – call it idiotic, if you will – conviction that something wonderfully exciting is about to happen.

I don't think one would call it exactly idiotic, but one does beg to differ on the subject of what may fairly be called wonderfully exciting.

COUNT ME OUT

The Challenge. By Phyllis Bottome (Faber, 1952).

The autobiographical spate continues. How fatally easy to write are the less reputable examples of this form of literature:

> Meantime, Uncle Walter had sold up the beloved Chelmsford house and had settled next to us in Collodeon Terrace. Well do I recall Mamma's displeasure when she heard of his imminent descent upon us. 'Uncle Wally' was definitely *persona non grata* with my parents, though to us girls he was a figure of enchantment and romance.
>
> Those who knew Croydon in the 90s will recollect Drugget's pastry-shop (now, alas, a fire-station). Hastening home from school, we would press our eager and, albeit, somewhat pink noses to the window, feasting our eyes the while on the dainties within. One day, my sister Ethel, greatly daring . . .

Miss Bottome's *Search for a Soul* took us through her first eighteen years of life. *The Challenge* carries us onwards to her early thirties, through years of ill-health to her meeting with Alfred Adler. These, we are told, 'are the years in which we must expose those hidden aims we have been choosing, and upon which we have built our life-plan, from our earliest childhood.' The exposing of Miss Bottome's hidden aims requires 400 pages and her memory is as disastrously efficient as that of Mrs. Robert Henrey; one is punch-drunk with reminiscence and already groggy in one's corner by the end of Round One. What do such writers do? Are vast diaries kept? How else does one remember that Paul said 'If you ever want to see me again I will come to you, but only on the condition that you accept me in advance as your lover. I do not mind seeing you in Rome, *en passant*, at Easter . . .'. Is it really profitable to know that the day before Auntie Lou's arrival, Paul cut some 'exquisitely designed' ham sandwiches, or that the Jeffersons' house-parlourmaid looked after the chickens?

Sometimes one barely knows where one is:

> Ernan was to meet us at Basle and to accompany us to Wesen and Tyrol, with or without his mother. Unfortunately, Mamma was at a little place called Baden not very far from Wesen – both being on the main line to Innsbruck – and she preferred to remain at Baden and *not* come to Wesen with us . . . She wished to continue the baths she had begun at Baden . . . I had to explain to my mother that Ernan could not escort us from Basle to Wesen; nor leave his mother alone at Baden.

Everything clear? Ernan turns up in the end (at Wesen), sporting a well-cut, pale grey, striped flannel suit, and no longer 'the forlorn boy I had parted from at the bottom of the Maloja Pass. In these few months Ernan had become a man,' and has a plan for joining the Japanese Navy.

Miss Bottome is a distinguished writer and, despite the suffocating blanket of detail, there is enjoyment here and there. But I would respectfully suggest that for the future she lays in a stout pair of scissors and learns how to snip.

QUEENING IT

The Queen Mother. By Helen Cathcart (W. H. Allen, 1965).
Mother of the Queen. By David Duff (Muller, 1965).

Literary clashes continue (why can't authors' future intentions be centrally registered somewhere?) and here are two Queen Mothers (collectively, a *goggle* of royalty) following hot on the heels of dual Jack the Rippers. Mrs. Cathcart, gently crowing about the special facilities accorded her 'in certain fields of inquiry', seizes her honey-pot and dives head-first in. On trips a 'Dresden china figure', 'the delectable Elizabeth', the 'born comedienne' to whom 'the echo of the distant drums of futurity sounded their soft whisper'. She grows up ('no longer

Girls will be Girls

the roseate pippin') and, of course, 'bourgeons into womanhood'. Eventually the widely loved, dumpy, pastel-coloured figure emerges, munching chocs, patting those horses, listening to the Dales, heading a conga line, fishing, hopping about in helicopters, piloting a Comet, and smiling, smiling, smiling. Mrs. Cathcart claims for her subject 'a complex and curiously reticent personality'. It would not seem so. Queen Mary thought her 'so pretty and engaging and natural', and the world has thought much the same ever since.

Alas, Mr. Duff too goes in for the phrase beautiful. As Duchess of York, she tried to help her stammering mate to get the words out faster, 'as if by the hypnotism of love she was calling the sounds from his throat.' We learn of 'the sparkle of her' and how, when swamped by large Canadians, 'the five feet two of her disappeared'.

Despite verbal unacceptabilities, both books will give pleasure to many and they do full justice to the remarkable record of selfless service. She has been equal to every test, some of them very severe ones, and charm, tact and hard work have rightly won her vast popularity. Do anti-royalists really long for the day when a PM's wife hands them their CBE's ('. . . and now do come and meet Harold')?

THE CROOKED BAT

CROOKED meaning not straight: not crooked meaning dishonest. It always seemed to me, as a schoolboy reluctantly playing cricket in the 1920s, that a straight bat, so highly prized by the experts, was in my case mere foolishness, sending the ball, when I managed to make contact with it, feebly back whence it had come. With a crooked bat there was at least a chance of deflecting the offensive weapon either to right or left and scoring a 'run'. To attempt to score anything at all may savour of self-advertisement but that was never my aim. My sights were not set on a ribboned coat or a captain's hand on my shoulder smote. The sole purpose of a run was to remove me, however briefly, from the end where the action was.

Cricket was a manly game. Manly masters spoke of 'the discipline of the hard ball'. Schools preferred manly games. Games were only manly if it was possible while playing them to be killed or drowned or, at the very least, badly maimed. Cricket could be splendidly dangerous. Tennis was not manly, and if a boy had asked permission to spend the afternoon playing croquet he would have been instantly punished for his 'general attitude'. Athletics were admitted into the charmed lethal circle as a boy could, with a little ingenuity, get impaled during the pole-vault or be decapitated by a discus and die a manly death. Fives were thought to be rather tame until one boy ran his head into a stone buttress and got concussion and another fainted dead away from heat and fatigue. Then everybody cheered up about fives. The things to aim at in games were fright and total exhaustion. It was felt that these, coupled with a diet that was only modestly calory-laden, would keep our thoughts running along the brightest and most wholesome lines. As a plan, this was a failure.

For cricket matches against other schools, the school pavilion was much in evidence. At my preparatory school, Stirling Court on the Hampshire coast, the pavilion smelt strongly of

Girls will be Girls

linseed oil and disinfectant and for its construction reliance had been largely placed on corrugated iron. Within could be found cricket nets and spiders and dirty pads and spiders and old team photographs and old spiders. There was also a bat signed by Hobbs which we proudly displayed to opposing players in an unconscious spirit of gamesmanship. But despite this trophy, a sad air of failure and decay pervaded the building. From its windows innumerable cricketing disasters had been witnessed: for example, our defeat by Dumbleton Park when our total score had been eight, three of which were byes. There had been, too, the shaming afternoon when our captain, out first ball, had burst into a torrent of hysterical tears.

But cricket did have one supreme advantage over football. It could be stopped by rain. Every morning at prayers, devout cricket-haters put up a plea for a downpour. As we were in England, our prayers were quite frequently answered, but nothing, nothing but the death of the headmaster could stop football. We could hardly pray for the headmaster, a nice man, to die. In rain, sleet, hail and lightning, shivering and shuddering and soaked to the skin, we battled on. Even in dense fog we kept at it, a shining example to Dartmoor working parties. But cricket was another matter, cricket was a more sensitive affair altogether, and if, as I fear, there is cricket in heaven, there will also, please God, be rain.

When the dread moment arrived and our side went in, I found myself, low down on the list, actually at the wicket and taking guard ('Leg stump, please'), and positively holding a bat. But held straight or crooked, sooner or later there would come the musical sound of skittling pegs and flying bails and I could remove myself and my pad and sit down. And once safely installed on a rug by the hedge and more or less out of sight, day-dreams took over.

I was badly stage-struck and many of my strange fancies consisted of meetings with Beatrice Lillie, Jack Buchanan and Gertrude Lawrence, all of them brightly dazzling stars whose personalities seemed infinitely more winning than those of the lacklustre adults with whom the expensive school fees were currently requiring one to associate. I gave Miss Lawrence tea at the Carlton on many occasions.

The Crooked Bat

Tea, Miss Lawrence?
Yes, please.
Milk, Miss Lawrence?
Yes, please.
Sugar, Miss Lawrence?
Four lumps, please.

When in course of time and much later in life, this particular daydream turned into reality, I was in no way surprised. I had become quite accustomed to the idea.

Tea, Miss Lawrence?
Yes please, dear.
Milk, Miss Lawrence?
Good God no!
Sugar, Miss Lawrence?
Don't be silly, darling! All I ask is that you should not be *silly*!

At Stirling Court there was an even more improbable day-dreamer than I, a remarkable boy called Williamson. He liked to pretend that he was the King, *a* King, any old King, graciously living incognito among us, and firmly incognito he looked with his blazer and grey shorts and grubby knees. It was possible to make him happy for hours by suddenly popping out from behind a tree and yelling 'Sire, Sire, I bring grievous news. Thirty of our stoutest bottoms have foundered off Gravesend.' There was then half a minute's pause for silent laughter. No schoolboy of twelve in those unsophisticated days was proof against the word 'bottom', even when signifying ship. Then Williamson would draw himself up to his full three foot eight and shriek in a piercing treble, 'Then go build ye fifty more, an' Sherwood Forest be stripped bare.'

Sometimes we invented a royal disaster so terrible and calamitous—suicide of the Queen, perhaps, theft of the Crown Jewels, bubonic plague at Westminster—that even Williamson was taken aback and could find nothing more regal to say than a dejected 'Oh *dear!*' On the soccer field, Williamson liked to play centre forward. He was King Harry leading us at Agincourt and bravely did we follow him, deep and offside into the enemy

Girls will be Girls

ranks with loyal shouts of 'God for Harry, England, Saint George and Williamson!' You would be right in thinking that we did not win a great many of our school matches.

When I was not day-dreaming myself into Shaftesbury Avenue, the existence or otherwise of a Supreme Being caused some perplexing youthful thoughts. Why, if God were All Good and All Powerful and All Sufficient, did he need to be quite so constantly Thanked? And Thanked for what seemed, as we gazed at the uninspiring, unchanging Sunday lunch, somewhat meagre blessings. In the season of mists and mellow fruitfulness, the mellow fruitfulness that most often came our way was beetroot. It did appear that, in comparison with God's other conjuring tricks, beetroot must rank as a minor achievement, especially when closely associated with vinegar.

And what was God up to? Why did my prayers (Freak Earthquake Destroys School) go completely unanswered? There was not even a disquieting rumbling sound to indicate that I had got through. Jesus seemed more approachable and I felt differently about Him, in spite of a daringly outspoken friend who pointed out that Christ had never had to undergo two of the most testing of human experiences, marriage and parenthood. Maintaining that there was no reason whatever to imagine Christ as devoid of humour, he invented a terrible pair of rude and undisciplined children for Him, Cynthia and Roland Christ, who roared about on motor-bicycles, got into every imaginable teenage pickle, and became a byword in Joppa.

At most schools in the 'twenties there was never any question of being let off cricket. The thought of asking not to play it never entered anybody's head. If it had, the consequences, at a public school anyhow, were clearly foreseeable. Suppose, let us say, a poetically-minded boy had announced that he wished to spend the afternoon writing an ode, he would have been immediately beaten (four strokes) by the Head of the House. Poetry was unhealthy stuff. Look at Byron. If the poet had been more specific and had said that he wanted to write an Ode to the Matron ('Oh Matron, when with grizzled head half bent with care, sweet ministrant of salve and unguent, breasting thy way defiant bust worn high . . .'), he would have been beaten (six strokes) by the Housemaster, and the poor (certainly) innocent

The Crooked Bat

(probably) Matron would have found herself writing to the scholastic agents, Chitty and Gale, for a new situation ('. . . said to have pleasant personality . . . prepared take sole charge . . . excellent "mixer" . . .'). If the embryo Shelley had said that he wished to write an Ode to the Captain of Cricket ('Oh Dennis, when with auburn head half bent with care . . .'), expulsion would have been considered, this extreme measure being subsequently watered down, after an infinity of scowls and threats, to a beating (eight strokes) by the Headmaster. These ceremonies used to take place at 9 p.m., the Headmaster sporting a dinner-jacket and being freshly vitamin-charged. The beatings were done, as usual, in the spirit of this hurts me more than you, which was said to be plenty.

When blessed rain had made the cricket pitches too sodden for activity, the obvious alternative, inactivity, was not permitted. We were herded together in the gymnasium. Sometimes there was boxing, that hideous and useless invention. Sometimes there was a pastime called Figure Marching. In Indian file we followed each other round strange geometrical figures, crossing and criss-crossing as instructed and forming patterns which would, no doubt, have looked pretty and interesting from a helicopter hovering above. It was before the days of helicopters.

More often than not, Physical Jerks were our lot, an unfortunate name implying as it does fits and starts and jolts and dislocations. The brochures which dealt with this form of exercise were copiously and incomprehensibly diagrammed. Dotted and arrowed lines and Fig. 6 seemed to prescribe patently absurd contortions. The instructors who steered us through them had chests like pouter-pigeons, crimson-veined faces and army connections. At the end of the lesson, it wasn't the done thing to invite the class quietly to stow away the medicine balls and falling mats that we had been using. Even this simple action had to have a military aura—'Mats away, *GO!* Balls away, *GO!*'

Though a crooked bat was frowned upon, to use the wrong, two-sides-of-a-triangle side was considered definitely illegal. Following my ingenious plan of deflecting the ball to one side or the other and then getting the hell out of it, I once made use

Girls will be Girls

of this wrong side of the bat and brought down upon myself a stream of abuse. The myth that this was, somehow, a dishonest practice, was one of many myths then current in schools:

—If you had a cracked lip and drank from a chipped cup, you would at once catch a disease that was as unmentionable as it was difficult to spell.
—The Eton College Officers' Training Corps was not allowed to wear the King's regulation khaki uniform as they had once, at an O.T.C. camp, bayoneted a boy to death. On Field Days didn't they turn out and turn up in a slightly outré pinkish material of their own devising? Well, then!
—Cold water came to the boil more quickly than hot water.
—Any actress employed upon the musical-comedy stage could be employed in a more private role for a sum of not less than fifty pounds. Didn't this vast extra intake of money explain those sumptuous-looking country houses in the soggier sections of the Thames Valley, and the photographs that went with them ('Off duty! Bimbo and self redesigning the bog garden.')?

At cricket there was never any thought of excusing those unfortunate enough to wear glasses. It was pre-contact lens days and short-sighted boys left their spectacles in their blazers in the pavilion. They stood, when batting, blinded by the sun and enfeebled by cruel Nature, peering uncertainly up the pitch in a hopeless attempt to see whence Nemesis was coming. They had to rely heavily on their other senses. Their sense of hearing supplied the thud and thunder of the bowler's cricketing boots, the wicket-keeper's heavy breathing (now coming from a lower angle as he crouched down in readiness) and the disagreeable whistling sound of the ball itself which indicated that it had been released and was on its way. Their sense of smell supplied the wind-borne unpleasantnesses of hot flannel, hot sock, hot boy, all of minimal value as directional guides. And their sense of touch told them, sharply and painfully, that the ball had arrived.

And here there was an unfairness. The boys in the First and Second XIs, fully sighted and well able to protect themselves, were provided with a contraption called a 'box', a snug and reinforced padded leather compartment worn about the crutch and into which they tucked, I assume, whatever came most easily to hand. It would have been considered a gross impertinence for any lesser player to plead for this protection. In the lower echelons, our genitals were expendable.

Fashions in cricket change like any others. At Stirling Court the important thing was what the ball would do when it struck the ground. It could go right or go left. It could do nothing special, or it could hit a tuft and shoot sharply upwards, a most unnerving ball. I understand, however, that nowadays the only matter of interest is what the ball does in the air. It seems that it 'swings' this way or that, though I cannot, alas, bring myself greatly to care.

It is sad but true that most of the best schoolboy cricketers of my day paid for their ephemeral glories with a lifetime of mediocrity. Cricketing fame can be fleeting. Who, for example, still remembers that Amy Johnson had one of her front teeth broken by a cricket ball and that she was the only girl at the Boulevard Secondary School, Hull, who could bowl over-arm?

* * *

Nothing was stranger at preparatory schools in the 1920s than the way in which a sudden spree was visited on the inmates. Without a word of warning, everybody up-anchored and shot off to somewhere else. At Stirling Court one summer's day a special treat was announced. We were all to go by charabanc, as a bus was then called, to watch a professional cricket match at Portsmouth. The outing meant, at least, no school work and even the more anti-cricket boys were in merry mood as we clambered on board. Williamson and I, deep in chat as was our custom, settled ourselves in. We were only mildly surprised to observe that the expedition was not being led by the games master but by a strangely-scented rotundity who taught Latin, was said to debauch the maids and pawn confiscated penknives, and survived but one shaky term. Off we went and on reaching the ground it was apparent that the game had been in progress for some time. Philip Mead, of whom even I had heard, was batting.

When we had found our seats, our first concern, after the hour's drive, was to make for the lavatory, an open-air and

Girls will be Girls

rather whiffy square construction of brick, conveniently close. As we hastened in, a solitary figure drew all eyes. In a corner, and facing outwards, an aged and decrepit clergyman was standing, smiling encouragement and wildly waggling. At our fairly tender years this was a startling spectacle and one hardly knew where to look. Where not to look was plain to all. Subsequent visits found him, hope on hope ever, still there and still at it. Not a cricket-lover, evidently.

In the charabanc *en route* for home, Mead's leg-glides gave place as a subject of conversation to our thoughts and views on the muddled divine. Could he have been, we charitably asked ourselves, quite right in the head? Unhinged in some way? Instinct told us not to discuss the matter with Matron when, that evening at bed-time, she inspected our toe-nails and indulged herself, after her lonely hours, with a few swift snippings.

Further astonishments completed a remarkable day. We were given two fried eggs each for supper, perched on a mound of sauté potatoes. This sumptuousness was without precedent and so entranced the school that the head boy automatically jumped up and gave three cheers for Mrs. Macdonald, the headmaster's deaf and remote wife, whose Buff Orpingtons had strained away to produce the main item of the feast.

While we were munching the eggs and discussing, naturally, the Reverend Whosit, the door burst open and the games master entered. Respectful silence fell. His lips could be seen to be trembling. He gulped. 'I want you all to know,' he said, 'that I alone was responsible for the charabanc starting so late this morning and for your missing part of the match. I can only apologise and ask for your forgiveness.' Silence continued; even I had stopped eating. 'But, although you may find it in your hearts to forgive me, I can never forgive myself.' Pressing a handkerchief to his wobbling mouth, he hurried out.

There now! What an exciting emotional outburst to round off the day! As it happened, neither Williamson nor I had noticed that the charabanc had started late. Happily seated in the very front of the conveyance, after shrieks of 'bags I!', we had been discussing the charms of Dorothy Dickson and he had at last agreed to swop his signed photograph of her for some

The Crooked Bat

rather pretty and ingenious cogwheels from my Number 4 Meccano set. As far as we were concerned, the charabanc need never have left at all.

To be honest, it must be confessed that the incident of the wonky clergyman was not entirely surprising to some of us. Preparatory schools at that time seemed each to have its quota of unmarried masters who were still looking about for Miss Right. Although it was difficult for them to marry on their miserable salaries, that was not, for all of them, the problem. Some of them were by nature looking about for Miss Right rather less vigorously than others. Dedicated paedophiles stalked the linoleum-covered corridors and, sensing a non-frosty reception, pounced. No boy who wasn't actually repellent could consider himself safe from an amorous mauling among the rows of pendant macintoshes. The purpose of these ungainly gymnastics was lost on the more naïve boys; they referred to the odd activities as 'romping', a verb which has since caught up with them. But I, an odious and knowing little giggling plumpness, was well aware of what was toward and realized that the merest show of cooperation would lead, sooner or later, in God's good time, somehow somewhere, to a sticky tribute. Bulls' eyes, for instance.

At school the best cricket players were loaded with honours and privileges throughout their brief years of glory, not the least of which was to see their names in print (a thrill at that age). The school magazine dutifully recorded their successes and faults.

Characters of the XI

H. R. J. VEREKER. Has 'skippered' excellently. His googlies were cleverly flighted and he has an outstanding action. His decision to promote G. J. B. Eyebright from the 'Colts' was fully justified.

G. J. B. EYEBRIGHT. An attractive bat who fully justified his promotion from the 'Colts'.

N. C. DE B. GASCOYNE. It is time he learnt not to nibble at off balls. Alert at silly mid-on but goes down rather sluggishly. Must use his head more.

Every cricket match, however dreary or disastrous, was fully

Girls will be Girls

reported. One dreadful term at Stirling Court when summer influenza had filled the dormitories and emptied the pavilion, we could only provide an XI to play against Dumbleton Park by pressing into service the eleven boys still on their feet. I had avoided summer influenza.

v. Dumbleton Park

Played at Stirling Court on July 3rd

Lost by nine wickets

'. . . and was quickly "yorked" for 2. Marshall, playing a little tentatively on 0, failed to survive a confident appeal for L.B.W. and assisted in the side's rapid collapse . . .'

School magazines also featured selections of heart-lifting news of Old Boys. These were mainly garnered from the letters that we periodically wrote to the headmaster. I had, doubtless, been boasting.

> C. F. JELLINEK has joined his father's smelting works in Bradford but has managed to keep up his interest in matters philatelic. Good old Jelly!
>
> P. N. HUFFKINS is still a flautist in the Bagshot 'week-end' orchestra and has become engaged to Miss Felicity Rollmops of 'Chatsworth', Station Crescent, Reading. Our warmest wishes for a tuneful 'duet'!
>
> A. MARSHALL has been broadcasting and has got to know Phyllis Monkman.

Names such as Jellinek and Huffkins are not comfortable ones for a boy to be landed with but in the end we tired of drawing attention to their oddity. Not so with some of the Christian names that lurked safely behind such initials as H.R.J. Occasionally it became necessary, when Common Entrance and School Certificate forms were being filled in, for a boy's full names to be revealed in the open classroom, and to the consternation of their owners out tumbled the Bertrams, the Herberts, the Jaspers, the Bellamys, the Clarences, the Augustuses, the Montmorencys, each of which was thought irresistibly droll when belonging to somebody else.

Although names were far from sacred at Stirling Court, two

things were: religious observances and parents. In the dormitories, those who wished could kneel unmolested to say their prayers, and photographs of our loved ones could be proudly displayed. Even the most mocking among us were respectfully silent when gazing at the framed likenesses of Mrs. Baughurst and Major Symington, smiling, pince-nezed and cabinet-size.

On one occasion, Mrs. Baughurst gave a vast picnic beanfeast for the entire school, goodies galore. She kindly came down herself for the affair and dispensed tea and iced lemonade, and smiles and chuckles to go with them. Her flowered dress reminded me of a cretonne sofa cover. She was enormously fat. Everything that could bulge, bulged. In due course, when we were all pleasantly replete, the head boy called for three cheers for Mrs. Baughurst, but later at supper he was heard to say that he really ought to have called for three chairs for Mrs. Baughurst. Though some of us thought this a witty quip and secretly admired it, it was generally found to be in very poor taste. It met with a chilly reception and for some days the head boy was not spoken to.

Humorists were not, as a general rule, encouraged. After the matchless *Bulldog Drummond*, which we all read once a term, our favourite reading was *Tarzan of the Apes*, by Edgar Rice Burroughs. At Stirling Court we had a boy called Edgar and when one day at lunch we had rice pudding, he seized his spoon and, plunging it into his heaped plate, said merrily, 'Edgar burrows in the rice.' Not particularly funny yet harmless enough and we laughed obligingly as we usually did (hoping for correspondingly jolly cackles when we ourselves were inspired to be witty). But the joke was by no means harmless in the eyes of the master at the head of the table. We were told to stop laughing and poor Edgar had to finish his lunch standing up (much more of a torment than it sounds) and was not allowed to bathe in the sea for a week, a typically bizarre and inappropriate scholastic punishment.

Another unfortunate humorous occurrence took place at Dumbleton Park, whither we had had to walk (two miles) in a surly, shuffling crocodile to watch yet another cricket match. A large, non-playing Dumbletonian, a well-known wag called Montefiore, politely sought to divert the visitors. He was wearing a tight white sweater and up inside it he inserted two cricket balls where a woman's breasts would, in his opinion, be. Looking very improbable, he then paraded mincingly up and down before our section of the spectators. He was a huge success. Our delighted laughter rang out, and some of us even applauded. As a spectacle, the cricket didn't stand an earthly.

At the close of play we scuffed our way back to Stirling Court and were just beginning our supper when the headmaster appeared, looking very far from genial. 'Which of you laughed at Montefiore and his disgusting exhibition?' There was a long, frightened silence. 'Stand up any boy who laughed at Montefiore!' More silence, and then a single victim courageously rose from his seat. It was Williamson, *noblesse oblige*. The rest of us, cowards to a boy, strove to look as though we had been deeply shocked by Montefiore.

Williamson was beaten just before evening prayers. By the time the summons came for him to go to the headmaster's study, he had transformed himself into the tragic person of Charles I going forth to his execution. Nothing could have been more regal as he strode from the room, patting a head here, a cheek there. 'Grieve ye not, good my peoples,' he said, passing solemnly through the door, 'and when I am gone, pray you, look to the Queen.' When he returned shortly after, rather pink in the face, Charles I had been forgotten. 'Only three, and they didn't hurt a bit.' It was characteristic of his generous nature to bear us no grudge for not owning up with him.

At my public school, you got off one afternoon's cricket a week by enlisting in the O.T.C. There were two parades a week and though the less lovely episodes of my years as a private are still vivid in the mind, it was just worth it. For the afternoon parade we struggled into some elaborate pieces of webbing and buckle in the armoury's dark recesses and were soon dressing by the right. Being on the plump side, I was difficult to align. I was the last to stop shuffling forwards or backwards, obligingly sticking out this or pulling in that and trying, in my friendly way, to help. There was then a good deal of marching about in fours and, chatting *sotto voce* to a neighbour, it was fatally easy to mishear words of command and to be discovered executing a faultless left incline while the others were busy right wheeling.

The Crooked Bat

One's little blunders were pointed out, in a stream of verbal discourtesies, by N.C.O.s and a pained look only drove them to further excesses.

Once a term the O.T.C. staged a mass outing known as a Field Day. More often than not in driving sleet from the east, we marched down to the railway station, the School Fife and Bugle Band doing, one supposes, its best to keep our spirits up. I wore a pair of thick and disapproved-of gloves to protect the chilblains that were an occupational risk of school life in bracing Northamptonshire.

With all the *joie de vivre* of slave labour bound for Siberia, we entrained and, in a third-class carriage, found ourselves gazing at a coloured view of The Promenade, Eastbourne. I had to insist on a corner-seat for, like some rare old wine, I did not travel well and nobody had yet invented Kwells. However, it was the work of a moment to rattle down the window and do what stern Nature demanded. Whenever we chugged through some wayside halt, I could be relied upon to leave behind a splashy greeting.

These activities were unpopular but all was forgiven and forgotten when we detrained near some blasted heath and marched bravely forth, clutching our sandwiches and spoiling for battle. The opposing force, after a train journey, tended to be either Rugby or Stowe. Sometimes we didn't even catch a glimpse of them, though the distant popping of blanks led one to believe they were somewhere about. When there was no train but a march of five miles, the enemy was invariably Uppingham. These, on one occasion, we did see. The leading sections met each other head on in the middle of a turnip field. The sight of the delicious bomb-like vegetable was too much and soon the nutritious roots were flying to and fro, scoring delightfully noisy direct hits. The officers seemed to miss the fun of the thing and, after we had downed turnips and dressed by the right ('Back a little, Marshall'), we were given a fearful wigging. But never mind. We hadn't had to play cricket.

* * *

If I seem to harp on cricket, it is only because in one's youth

Girls will be Girls

there was such a terrible amount of it. I estimate that during my passage through the 1920s, 2,000 hours, or about eighty-four days and nights, or twelve whole weeks of my life were spent, longing to be elsewhere, in flanelled gloom in the middle of a field. But no, I am wrong. Luckily enough it was not always in the middle of the field but more towards the side of it. Having, at Stirling Court, proved myself a butterfingers at anything calling for speedy action and initiative near the batsman and wicket, I spent a comparatively peaceful two years in a position well known at preparatory schools but without, I feel, any official recognition. I refer to the key post of Long Stop. It is to be found immediately behind the wicket-keeper (at Stirling Court, the wicket was kept, naturally, by Williamson) towards the boundary of the field of play and it has much to recommend it.

Socially it was agreeable as it allowed you to pass the time of day with friends enjoying nougat nearby, but its chief charm lay in the fact that there was only one chance in five of you ever being drawn into the unlovely cricketing picture. The ball when bowled might hit the batsman, the batsman might hit it, it might hit the wicket, it might hit the wicket-keeper. When it missed all these hazards and came rolling towards you, you found yourself in the very thick of the game. Old hands like myself, however, felt no need to panic. The grass in the outfield was by nature long and lush and if it had not recently been mown, there was a good chance of the ball coming to a halt before it even reached you. No point in meeting trouble halfway. Ignoring unmannerly shouts to run, you waited for the ball to come to rest and then, hurrying briskly forward, you picked it up and threw it in, thus skilfully preventing the batsmen from crossing for the fifth time.

At school we faced the tyranny of cricket, and of all games, in the same uncomplaining way that we faced surds, fractions, Canada's exports, Euclid, Tasmania's imports, and the Hundred Years' War. It was all part of the scholastic merry-go-round, part of Life's rich pattern. Daily we put on those hot and unsuitable cricketing togs, the bags supported by a school belt with snake clasp. On our heads we placed those enormous shapeless grey felt bonnets without which small boys were

The Crooked Bat

thought to succumb instantly from sunstroke, and out on to the field we trooped for a generous three hours of the national game.

Beneath a tree stood the visible scoring apparatus, a selection of white numbers on sheets of black tin hung on a discarded blackboard and mysteriously known as the Tallywag. The boys who worked this were a sort of walking wounded, boys recovering from boils or headaches or lunch or asthmatic attacks and they had behind them a long tradition of indolence and lack of cooperation. They lay on their stomachs chewing wine-gums and reading another chapter of *The Black Gang*. When they tired of that, they would just aimlessly hit each other for five minutes or so. From time to time, a despairing cry of 'TALLYWAG' would reach them from the pitch, and they would then reluctantly change the tin plates to a score that was possibly accurate to the nearest ten. At the end of play, they were allowed by old custom to leave the Tallywag showing a somewhat improbable result to the game (999 for 1, last man 998).

At public schools, the summer term ended with a week at an O.T.C. camp. To get to the camp we, of course, entrained, and after prolonged discomfort reached a tented enclosure, often at one or other of those trying Tidworths (Park or Pennings). The moment we arrived, and with not a second to freshen up or take a restorative, we were barked at by the red-tabbed regular officer in command ('Here to work . . . no shilly-shallying . . . put your backs into it . . .'), addressed by the padre ('See you at Church Parade . . . sing up . . . put your backs into it') and given by the medical officer some superfluous hygienic hints. We were then free to inspect our roomy quarters.

Not much caring for the feel of blankets upon the bare skin, I had had constructed at home a sleeping-bag of old sheets. This comforting device caused unaccountable rage (jealousy, I can only suppose) but nobody could think of any reason for withdrawing it. But, sheeted or not, sleep under canvas was not easily come by. To discourage conversation, the officers went about thwacking with their sticks on the tent sides but all that this noisy show did was to awaken the earwigs. Sensing intruders, they scurried up to the top of the tent-pole and then,

Girls will be Girls

with a do-or-die abandon, hurled themselves down on to one's face. After the last wave had gone in, the ants took over. And when their work was done, the rain, in a gentle patter, began.

For the more sensitive digestions, the camp food was chancy. It was prepared without the hand of love in black apparatus that had the look of being salvage from the Crimea. Not that the officers were indifferent. Indeed, they were for ever bursting in at meal-times and inquiring whether there were any complaints. One boy, not realizing that this was a purely formal question requiring nothing but glum despair by way of answer, once drew attention to some culinary mishap or other—a dead mouse in the stew or some such bagatelle. Everyone was very shocked (not, of course, about the mouse) and nobody complained again.

The washing arrangements were very far from ideal, and about certain other arrangements I prefer not to speak. By way of drawing attention officially to their unsavoury primitiveness, they were usually burnt down on the last night of camp and provided a cheering spectacle. An opportunity was made in the morning for us to be reprimanded about this, after we were, naturally, nicely in line ('Up a little, Marshall'), but at the final breakfast nobody bothered to ask us if we had any complaints for how could we have? We were going home.

The admirable length of the summer holidays prevented one from thinking very much about the forthcoming winter term and what lay ahead in the form of Rugby football. But Rugby football did have one small silver lining—you could occasionally lie down and take a short rest. Of course, it wasn't called lying down and resting. It was known as 'falling on the ball' to stop the opposing forwards dribbling it, and it was an entirely brave and praiseworthy action. It usually caused a loose scrum to be formed over your inert body and so your resting period was sometimes quite prolonged. The ground might be damp but exertion was momentarily over. Pleasantly relaxed and outstretched, one could ponder on this and that—the universe, the eternal mysteries, or which delicacy was being prepared for house supper at 7 p.m. I did a lot of falling on the ball. 'Well fallen, Marshall' a kindly captain would cry, drawing attention to my selfless pluck. While lying down one sometimes got a

The Crooked Bat

football boot in the face but then everything here below has its price.

In the summer holidays there were still a lot of games. Parents tended to think that juvenile social life could not move happily forward without games. And so out of doors we played tennis and croquet and golf and badminton, and indoors there was bridge, bezique, halma, chess, happy families, mah-jongg, and a pencil-and-paper game called Consequences which provided pleasurable fantasies such as 'Stanley Baldwin met Gladys Cooper in the Taj Mahal'.

I rather enjoyed the tennis parties. For these the sun seemed always to shine. They began at 3 p.m. and everybody was dressed entirely in white, though ladies were permitted a coloured Suzanne Lenglen bandeau to keep their shingles in position, and the belts that supported the gentlemen's flannels could, at a pinch, be dark blue. On the very tick of three, you alighted from your bicycle, shook hands with your hostess ('*How* you've shot up, Arthur! School seems to suit you!') and then, with the other guests, you stood gazing at the tennis court which old Hawker had freshly marked out with wavering hand and tottering feet.

In those days, the tennis posts were not such reliable contrivances as they are now and on really damp courts (vicarage ones were, for some reason, especially sodden) the softness of the earth and the tension of the net caused the posts to lean amorously towards each other. Geometrically, this lowers the height of the net. Here there was no question of a white band in the middle to keep the net down. The whole problem was how to keep it up and it was quite in order to prop the centre of the net with a sort of metal prong. If there were no prong, an agonized and embarrassed daughter of the house might sometimes whisper to her mother that she thought the net was sagging. The reply was firm and simple: 'Erica, it is *not* sagging. Now, hurry up all of you, you're wasting precious sunlight.'

If you were fortunate, you would find upon the tennis court six tennis balls, never one more, and frequently one less. They had been in service since the beginning of the season and were now dark green in colour and, though light in weight from

Girls will be Girls

constant use, were strangely reluctant to bounce very high. Sometimes they had been smeared with tennis-shoe whitening so that the first few shots covered you with exciting explosions of white dust. Then they went dark green again. On a table in a shady spot (under the cedar, if cedar there were) stood the refreshment, a large jug of home-made lemonade, than which there is nothing nicer, covered with a piece of butter-muslin to discourage flies and hemmed with beads to keep it in place. There were deck chairs scattered about and a rug or two (a large bundle of rugs sometimes turned out to contain an elderly relation, wheezing encouragement), and some of those old-fashioned racquet presses that look like mediaeval contraptions for helping reluctant persons to speak up.

The number of players for one court was usually ten, so you had to get as fond of sitting down and talking as of playing. When the main body of guests had arrived ('I think poor old Gregory must have got a puncture'), and the hostess had made mention of what a lovely day they had brought with them, she would then say 'Now, how will you play? Who'll start?' This was the cue for everybody to put on a condemned look and shout simultaneously 'Oh no, I'd much rather sit out. Please, Mrs. Bancroft, truly.' In the end, four players were chivied on to the court, where they all set up a wailing moan of 'Well, I must be given the best player because I'm absolutely putrid, no really I am.'

The tennis playing itself was a sort of ritual. It bristled with ceremony and complications and observances and rules of behaviour. For example, if you did a particularly good service, what one might gaily call an 'ace', the accepted thing was to assume that your opponent wasn't looking and hadn't prepared himself. 'I say, were you ready?' you called, to which the invariable answer was 'Yes, but not for that!' Merry chuckles. If a ball came down the centre of the court, or anywhere near it, you and your partner both screeched 'Yours, partner' and then leapt away from the ball as though it were a hand grenade just fizzing to a conclusion. To rush towards such a ball would have been to lay yourself open to the serious charge of 'poaching'. Poaching wasn't popular; poachers' names became known and then poachers weren't asked again.

The Crooked Bat

Shots that looked as though they had fallen just out of court had to be sportingly announced as having fallen just in ('No, honestly Helen, I'm quite quite sure'). Not a moment passed without some sort of comment from somebody and the air rang with 'Good shot', 'Hard luck', 'Well tried' and 'Oh I say, *I* didn't think it was coming over either'. If there was a spirited rally, with the ball changing sides as often as five or six times, somebody was sure to give a jolly cry of 'Why go to Wimbledon?' Shots of unintentional brilliance, such as a dazzling backhand sliced smash off the racquet handle and part of one's thumb, had to be apologised for for minutes on end. When a ball was carelessly struck and flew out of court and into the flowers, that was the signal for all the spectators to rise, to say in unison 'All right, I'll get it', and then to move off in a sort of mass migration and start trampling down the lupins.

Play halted during this manœuvre while all the players gathered at the nearest point behind the stop-netting and yelled conflicting instructions: 'Further in, Cyril', '*Much* more to your right', 'Now, Muriel, walk straight towards me'. If a ball was lost during the last hour of play, the hostess would say 'Never mind, we'll look for it later', which explains why there were sometimes five balls instead of six.

The first set after tea (home-made cakes, huge slices of wafer-thin bread-and-butter, ginger snaps, Earl Grey) was always a men's four, the ladies being thought to be too distended with macaroons to be able to move with any ease or pleasure. So they sat out and dabbed their mouths with the handkerchiefs that had been tucked into the gold bangles which they wore just above the left elbow.

Later on, the master of the house would sometimes return from work and could occasionally be coaxed by his wife into taking part: 'I think that if we spoke *really* nicely to Herbert he might be persuaded to join you in a final set.' Loyal cries of 'Hooray!' from the guests, and ten minutes or so later the genial and beflanelled host would reappear from the house shouting something comical such as 'Lead on, Macduff', or 'Will one of you young chaps lend me a bat?' And then, after his efforts had turned him a deep and rather worrying purple colour, and despite everybody's co-operation he had lost the set

Girls will be Girls

6–0, there would start up the usual preparations for goodbye—'Just look at the time', 'I must really fly: we've got Aunt Honor coming to dinner'. And in a flurry of thank-yous, it was on to one's bicycle and away. And if one hadn't poached, there would probably be another tennis party the very next day.

*   *   *

Even the most high-spirited boys experienced a feeling of wretchedness and doom when returning to Stirling Court for the winter term. We were as dejected as Mrs. Macdonald's Michaelmas daisies which by now were covered in cobwebs and sea-mist and general dankness and were the only one of Nature's vegetable wonders currently visible from the classroom windows. Williamson himself, seldom one to flag, looked listless, even in the year when he had returned from the summer holidays with a splendid new fantasy. He imagined that the entire royal family had been annihilated by some giant *machine infernale* which had exploded at a royal wedding. After diligent search, the authorities discovered that the nearest surviving relative (2,845th in succession) was a Mrs. Denise Harrison, living in somewhat questionable circumstances in Maida Vale (in a hotel where men stayed for only quite short periods of time) and no stranger to strong waters. She comes to the throne and is speedily known as Queen Denise the Damned. Constantly drunk, she appears at odd hours on the balcony, blowing kisses and making unsuitable gestures. At the Coronation service, she drinks off the Communion wine in one gulp, demands cocktails as a chaser, waves tipsily from the coach and, reaching out a hand, drags into it a Scots guardsman and draws the curtains. After a short while, his trousers are ejected. She dies, hopelessly dotty and intoxicated, while trying to fondle the Archbishop of Canterbury. This pleasurable improbability did cheer us all for a few days.

When the first endless fortnight had come to a close, it was only the beginning of October, with two full months and most of December still to go. Life was a drab procession of dreadful Latin and French irregular verbs (among them, poor old *ouïr*, of which so little seemed to exist). The French sentences we translated were always either full of unreality ('This rake is mine but whose hoes are those?') or non-sequiturs ('My hands are very sore but I am richer than you think').

Still, there were always the new boys to persecute and bombard with cricketing riddles:

> Who was the first cricketer in the Bible?
> Don't know.
> St. Peter.
> Why?
> He stood up before the eleven and was bold.
> Oh.
>
> Who bowled fewest balls in the Bible?
> Don't know.
> The eunuchs.
> Why?
> They hadn't any.
> Oh.
>
> Why is a tie like a telescope?
> Don't know.
> Because it pulls out.

On this occasion the 'Oh' was more of a shriek for when the miserable boy's tie was pulled out, it was frequently attached to his shirt by a tie-clip so that the front part of the shirt came out too. And, deeply humiliated and unaccustomed to this kind of jollity, he dared not blub until he had got safely into a lavatory.

To savour more fully the pleasure of not having to play cricket, we would often run over the high points of the summer season. One year the sports' master had been removed, not for any of the usual reasons but with appendicitis. His replacement seemed not to care for cricket and to do nothing but sit in the shade and read and this withdrawal gave a boy called Mould a chance to shine. He was very small and rather weasel-like and he had become an expert bowler of high-speed sneaks, varying them with those balls of alarmingly high trajectory that come dropping out of the sky like a bomb. Neither of these deliveries is recommended by the cognoscenti, but then neither of them is actually illegal and as the gentleman in the shade seemed neither to notice nor mind, Mould opened our bowling for a full six weeks. Success was immediate. To stop the sneaks (it was impossible to score from them), the very bottom of the bat had to be used. This frequently sent a painful, stinging tremor up the bat and the batsman's arms, in which case Mould would bowl the next ball instantly, usually capturing a valuable wicket. On dazzlingly sunny days, Mould's bombs took fine toll of the blinded batsmen, either in wickets or in injuries. In this manner, we had been able to trounce our dreaded rivals, Dumbleton Park, both 'at home' and 'away', while Westcliff went down like nine-pins (a total of 7, and three boys in tears).

And in addition to Mould, there was always Williamson, who went in first wicket down and whose regal deportment with the bat constantly demoralized opposing bowlers. His haughty mien put one in mind of Henry VIII and it was his habit, while the bowler was thundering down for his first ball, to cry out 'just one moment, please', and then effect a small adjustment to his clothing. But alas, when the sports' master returned, minus appendix, all was discovered, we were reprimanded for unsporting behaviour, and poor Mould was demoted to the second eleven.

One November day, another surprise treat was announced. Owing, we were told, to the kindness of the ever-generous Mrs. Baughurst, we were to be shown a film in the village hall, where there was a proper projector. As the hall was in full use most afternoons (and for adult film performances in the evenings), the little excitement had to be arranged for the morning, which meant an hour or two less work. A treat indeed. The music mistress, Mrs. Wakefield, had kindly consented to seat herself at the upright while the silent film was unreeling and give us of her best.

On thinking over the disaster afterwards, we came to the conclusion that Mrs. Baughurst had trustingly put herself in the hands of the hall manager and had requested a film suitable for young persons, and the manager, to save money and trouble, had merely decided to show the film destined for that evening, which he probably hadn't yet seen. So, after a Pathé Gazette and a short travel film (Hungary, jerking up and down in down-

The Crooked Bat

pours of rain), the main feature began, to a tuneful selection by Mrs. Wakefield from *Merrie England*.

The film was called *Frailty, Thy Name Is* . . . and it was set in the depths of the English countryside. There were three chief characters—Farmer Giles (generously bewhiskered), Mrs. Giles (considerably younger than her rustic mate), and Bob, the farm hand (considerably younger than his employer). Bob lived with the Giles and took all his meals with them and one did just wonder why, instead of getting on with the plentiful home fare, he was spending quite so much time leering at Mrs. Giles from behind a cottage-loaf.

AND THUS FOR SOME WEEKS THE BUSY FARM LIFE CONTINUED

said the caption, and there they all were, milking cows, churning butter, feeding chickens and collecting eggs. Just a peaceful bit of old England.

AND SO TO THE NIGHT WHEN DESTINY WAS TO WRECK THREE LIVES

it ran, and the night began with a frightful storm, with trees being blown down and every farmhouse window banging. In the morning, it was found that a section of the farmhouse thatch had come adrift and, mounting a ladder to repair it, Farmer Giles missed his footing, crashed heavily to the ground, writhed for several minutes, was examined by the doctor and carried to bed where he lay motionless and with a displeased expression, Mrs. Giles being very solicitous and patting pillows.

I BE NO USE TO THEE, LASS. I CAN MOVE NEITHER HAND NOR FOOT

Nor anything else, one was given to understand, for Bob now increased his appalling leers, and Mrs. Giles, who at first had not noticed them, now started noticing them like anything.

Seated at the piano, Mrs. Wakefield was out of sight of the screen and had throughout been unaware of the nature of the drama that was unfolding itself. She specialized in what was then a popular piece of pianoforte virtuosity—the *valse brillante*. This was an ordinary *valse* but with the addition of great runs and tremendous trills and bangings and much crossing of the hands. She had rightly reserved a few of the best of these for the last reels of the film and by now she was in fullest flood and producing a delightful cascade of thrilling and cheerful melody.

But what was this? Mrs. Giles, as slim as a rake to start with, was visibly increasing in size, especially round the lower middle section, with Bob leering like a maniac and Farmer Giles looking grumpy and narrowing his eyes at his wife whenever she took him up his lunch. And then, unknown either to Bob or Mrs. Giles (they were clearing out the hay-loft, or so they said), Farmer Giles hobbled painfully from bed and fetched his shot-gun, concealing it in a bedroom cupboard.

For some time now, there had been anxious mutterings in the hall's rear seats, where the staff were drinking in the entertainment. Now one heard people walking about and suddenly the film flickered away into darkness and the hall lights were switched on. Mrs. Wakefield brought her current *valse brillante* to a reluctant close and we were all told to walk back to Stirling Court. There, after lunch, the Headmaster said that, by some mistake, we had been shown a film that was really only meant for 'grown-ups' and which we wouldn't have enjoyed (we had seen most of it) and would we please not mention the matter in our Sunday letters home, other than the bare fact that there had been a film. Doubtless something soothing and false was written to Mrs. Baughurst but we were accustomed to such prudery and concealments. Williamson never let us forget that when, in his first term and during some dormitory horseplay (Drake on the bowling-green), he had broken a *pot de chambre*, the item had appeared on his end-of-term bill as 'Large teacup: 5/–'.

And thus for some weeks the busy winter term continued. Every month we had our hair cut by a hairdresser from Southsea and his lady assistant, whose unlovely task it was to shampoo our heads. For this, we repaired to the bathroom and, with towels round our necks to sop up the trickles, we bent our heads over the side of a bath. This, naturally, gave Williamson a chance for yet another Charles I decapitation performance, much to the lady's irritation ('Oh you *silly* boy!'), but he pardoned her with a regal gesture and then, to show that he had other strings to his bow, he would give his famous impression of José Collins singing 'Love will find a way'—a deafening

The Crooked Bat

treble rendering that the entire school, except for the staff, found entrancing.

One evening, in just such a winter term, something took place that, unknown to me at the time, was to give an unusual purpose to my life. The headmaster announced that there was to be a school debate. What a debate was had to be explained to most of us. The motion before us was something to do with public transport. The debate began. Masters spoke. Boys droned on about this and that. Probably mishearing some debating point, or idiotically misunderstanding it, I got up and said something or other, and everybody laughed, and laughed really quite loudly. I blushed, thinking I had been stupid, but I was very far from being displeased. Golly, what an *agreeable* sound, I thought, and I had, however unwittingly, caused it. I had suddenly become consciously aware of laughter and since that day I have always tried to go where laughter was, to seek laughter out, to impede laughter as little as possible, to have as friends people who could make me laugh (they have been extremely kind), to read books that provoke, either intentionally or otherwise, laughter, to see plays intended to provide laughter. I am aware that as a major aim in life this has been frivolous and petty and, maybe, rather contemptible and that I should have been worrying about the state of the world, the human condition, and poverty and famine and misery. But I am afraid that I haven't been and, I must confess, it's been great fun.

ERIC BROUGHT UP TO DATE

1959

It was obvious why cricket appealed so strongly to the members of school staffs. They could enjoy at least three hours rest while it was going on, in the certainty that none of us were able to get into bad trouble. Conspicuous in white and thoroughly *en évidence* in the middle of a field, it was not possible either to smoke or to drink. Nobody could run away, or peer at saucy magazines, or rag the French master. Further juvenile infelicities could only be achieved by real ingenuity and dedication.

In schools where little cricket was played, the lengthy summer afternoons simply invited serious scrapes. It is true that on the cover of the 1903 edition of Frederic W. Farrar's deathless masterpiece *Eric, or Little by Little*, there is a likeness of a youthful cricketer (straight bat), and on page 64 Eric certainly *says* that he is off to play cricket, but it was only an excuse to avoid having to admire the pretty sea-anemone collection lovingly formed by his young brother, little Vernon. Cricket does not seriously appear again until page 335, and then only because Eric, going full tilt down the slippery slope to perdition and finding himself short of cash, helps himself to a fiver from the cricket subscription box.

Dean Farrar's preoccupations were with higher things than cricket. Had this saintly man lived in the present day, it is tempting to wonder how his immortal tale might have gone. Let us then try, retaining of course the Dean's style, rounded yet trenchant, forceful yet mellow, and his kindly habit of addressing his characters and urging, nay *willing*, them to adopt a different course of action to the one on which they are so disastrously set. Is he ever successful? No, he is not, but like a sturdy Christian, he battles on.

Eric Brought up to Date

Roslyn School on an afternoon of high summer. My pen is inadequate indeed to do justice to the supreme beauty of it all – the tall, stately buildings, the majestic lines of the laundry (Togger to each and every Roslynite), the daisy-dappled greensward, and the golden sunlight that fell like a benison through the ambrosial foliage of the limes, their pale blossoms murmurous with bees. In their grateful shade, Eric Williams, in jeans and a T-shirt, was idly flipping through the school library copy of *Last Exit to Brooklyn*. Yawning loudly, he tossed the book to his friend, Montagu.

'Here you are, Hank. It all seems pretty old hat to me.'

Oh Eric, Eric! You, a youth on the threshold of life, already a prey to ennui? The nuclear age holds such a wealth of treasures to cherish and admire. Look about you, boy! Look up, look down, look sideways, look out! Oh Eric, Eric!'

'Good Lord! What's the old man doing here?'

A portly figure was approaching. Dr. Rowlands was paying one of his rare visits to the school. As befits a modern educationist, the headmaster expended the major part of his time on the public weal. No TV showing of *Come Again* was complete without his pleasant sincerity and weighty scholarship. He was the bulwark, nay, the main stanchion of *What Am I Holding?* on the radio. There were Brains Trusts here and symposia there, on all of which he lavished the rich fruits of his cultivated taste. The selfless activity brought him publicity, fame even. It also brought him fees.

In matters scholastic, the Doctor was something of a visionary. Irksome restrictions had been well-nigh abolished, dress was optional, classes voluntary, and the headmaster and Mrs. Rowlands delighted in being 'Jumbo' and 'Sybil' to all but the most junior.

Pausing to shake off two fourth-formers who were clamouring for autographs, Dr. Rowlands sauntered towards the tree-girt pair.

'Ah, Eric and Hank. How nice.'

'Good heavens, Jumbo, we thought you were at Lime Grove.'

'No, that's tomorrow. I've just nipped down for the day to see how the Appeal is coming along. How right we were to ask for £600,000. It *looks* well. The higher the sum, the better the school.'

Old Roslynites in all corners of the globe had been circulated and right nobly had they answered the call. Cheques, postal-orders and books of stamps, some of them virtually unused, had

Girls will be Girls

poured in from hill-station and bungalow, from igloo and wigwam, each loyal alumnus counting it a joyous task to help restore, embellish, and, in certain cases, demolish chosen sections of the beloved fabric.

'Yes. It seems to be going pretty well. £8,992 to date. It begins to look as though Sybil can get started on her new wing. We're a bit cramped, you know. The Bishop has to share our bathroom. A Bishop oughtn't really to have to share anything. Well, I must get on with some work,' and away he strolled to his study, emerging shortly after to fix a notice upon the door: DO NOT DISTURB. ANSWERING FAN-MAIL.

Scarcely had he gone when a slight figure in a neat dark blue pinstripe could be espied hastening purposefully towards Williams and Montagu, the sunlight glinting fiercely on the polished horn-rims.

'God! Here's that ghastly little drip, Russell.'
'Oh Eric, Eric, thank goodness I've found you!'
'Well, Russell?'
'Do please call me Edwin!'
'I can't. It's such a bloody silly name. What do you want?'

Russell's pained eyes fell for a moment on the library book and, colouring instantly, he looked hastily away.

'Well, Eric, I was just now on my way to extra coaching with Mr. Rose for the Moulding Bursary. It's at Keble, you know, and only open to intending ordinands. And I saw your brother, poor little Verny . . .'

'His name's Vernon.'
'Vernon, then. I saw him with . . . with Ball!'

I hurry over a part of my narrative inconceivably painful. Tremble, tremble, reader, at the name of Ball! Ball, he whose vile influence was spreading like some noisome grey lichen over those hallowed walls that weren't too flaky to take it. Ball, the forefront fighter in the devil's battle, he of the mean disposition and feeble intellect. Down on your knees, reader, and pray, pray for Ball!

'Well, I don't care what friends Vernon chooses to make. I think he's done rather well, actually; Ball's father's at Harwell. He might be able to wangle something decent for us when we leave.'

Oh Eric, Eric! Art thou not thy brother's keeper, guardian (while thy parents are in Bermuda) of those baby lips, that pure young heart? Thoughtfulness for others – this lesson, worldly

Eric Brought up to Date

'Thanks very much, Sybil. I'd love to.'

'Oh, *goody*!'

Some two hours later, the head boy knocked at Dr. Rowlands' drawing-room door.

'What is it, Julian? As you see, I'm rather busy.'

'I thought I'd better just let you know, Jumbo, that Russell's got himself cut off on the Stack.'

This forbidding mass of isolated schist was an impressive feature of Roslyn Bay.

'What a little pest! But is the Stack totally immersed at high tide?'

'All but ten feet of it.'

'In that case, what are we worrying about?' boomed the Doctor genially. 'Russell may find himself a surprised winner of the Rumbould Physical Endurance Chalice. Why, I might even get him an interview on 24 *Hours*. Now then, four diamonds doubled, is it? Down you go, partner.'

Mrs. Rowlands, a proud dummy, spread out her hand.

'*Really*, Sybil! Where are the two quick tricks?'

'Oh dear! I thought my void in clubs . . .'

'Rubbish!' said the Doctor loudly, revealing for a pleasing moment the man behind the cathode-ray tube.

Russell's funeral took place the following Friday, the mournful event being somewhat hurried on so as not to form an inconvenient clash with Saturday's cricket fixture against the National Provincial Bank.

Weep for him, Eric, weep for him! In salt tears, freely and sincerely shed, thou mayst wipe away thy indifference and neglect of this thy loving, pure young friend. Be not afraid, boy. Manly tears are no disgrace. Even Generals have been known to weep, when the reviewers were spiteful. Shed them, dear muddled lad, shed them!

And that night Eric's pillow was wet. A sudden storm, aided by an open window, had completely soused the freshly laundered napery.

CHRISTMAS REVIEWS OF BOOKS FOR GIRLS

1951

ODSBODIKINS

Blondel the Minstrel. By Allen W. Seaby (Harrap).
The Armourer's House. By Rosemary Sutcliff (Oxford University Press).
The Gauntlet. By Ronald Welch (Oxford University Press).
Path to Glory. By Showell Styles (Faber).

A VARIED Historical Panorama leaves one no space for an informative preamble. To work!

In *Blondel the Minstrel* we are in the world of white palfreys, frumenty, quilted overshirts, plague-purifications, baldrics, silken mutches and women called Adalberta. Blondel practises on his hand-harp ('*Tum-tumti-tum. Tum-tumti-tum.* That's the way it goes, Blondel') and becomes the musical rage of Venice with his 'high-class chansons of courtly love' and his violet eyes (' 'Tis an angel, surely'). Count Bertrand de Born introduces him to Richard Coeur de Lion, himself a talented troubadour ('he gets it from his poor old mother') and Blondel has instantly to provide a sample of his gifted twanging: 'come hither, lad, and trill me the first ditty which comes into your curly-haired pate. Do not be nervous', he kindly adds, 'I shall not eat you', and Blondel's light tenor ('his voice had broken some time back') booms agreeably round the stonework.

Richard is preparing 'a crusade on the grand plan' with Archbishop Baldwin and other hotheads but Blondel breaks a leg and can't go along: Queen Eleanor is a bracing sick-visitor ('Drop that crestfallen air, Blondel'). Blondel is well out of it as 'Crusading in Palestine was no joke' and at any moment you might get bitten by a camel or stop an infidel's arrow in the fleshy part of the leg just below your gambeson: 'and it *was* hot'. Richard is the life and soul, relieves the garrison at Joppa 'without even troubling to put on his mailed shoes', and, laid low by ague, gamely pots Saracens from the prone position. Blondel winds up as a Benedictine (Father Ambrose) and 'the head of the scriptorium' takes down from dictation his chansons and plaints (*Tum-tumti-tum* again).

The Armourer's House is so rich in Tudor detail and fine holland shifts, rook pies, silver hawk-bells, larded capons, dandelion wine, fennel poultices, rushlights, musk and bee-balm posies that one begins to long for homely things like Football Pools, road-drills and Heinz's baked beans. Into all this comes Tamsyn Caunter, 'tittuping' up from Bideford to stay with her cousins Piers, Giles, the Almost-Twins, Beatrix, and the golden-headed, cornflower-blue eyed Littlest (' "Littlest loves you," said Littlest'). Nothing very striking happens except in Tamsyn's highly emotional *entrailles*: first she feels 'desperately low in her inside' and starts to 'ache deep down inside her': then she becomes 'queer and screwed-up in her inside' and suddenly senses 'something hard and bright in her inside'. The sight of Piers at archery practice makes her 'quite pink inside' and Uncle Martin's visit causes her inside to 'sway gently up and down'.

The children visit a Wise Woman (Wart-charming and Shingles a Speciality) who, with her 'and what do 'e want wi' old Tiffany Simcock?' must be a Starkadder forebear. She gives them hyssop honey ('There 'bain't none so sweet'), spots Tamsyn as a fellow Devonian, advises against picking rampion at Midsummer, Ruth Drapers her way through her borage, wormwood, memilot, bergamot, elecampane and cummin, and has a good word for the Druids ('but they weren't no wiser than old Tiffany Simcock, my days, no!'). Tamsyn is quoted as saying loverly, beasterly, and miser-rubble, and ripe gooseberries are 'bursty-soft' and figs 'slishy'. Prolonged reading has the effect of a double helping of cherry conserve pasty thickly daubed with honey (Simcock's Best Hyssop of course).

In *The Gauntlet*, Peter Staunton has a Moberly-and-Jourdain translation back into the fourteenth century and finds himself

Girls will be Girls

having a lesson in table manners from the Lady Marian: don't dip your tench in the salt: don't let gravy trickle on to your cote-hardie: don't blow your nose with the eating hand (the Lady Marian obligingly demonstrates on to the rushes). There are liripipes, peregrine falcons, butts of Malmsey (at this period full of nothing but Malmsey), groats, Bends Sinister, and a witch (Blodwen Rees). The Lord Roger togs up in woollen drawers, haqueton, hauberk, sollerets and demi-jamberts and has a spirited joust with Fulk Fitz-Osborne, finally flooring him with a deft thwack on the bascinet. A recommendable book, if only for a mouth-watering recipe for pork liver balls (clutch with two fingers and thumb only: appreciative eructations are *de rigueur*).

Path to Glory is a series of episodes concerning Admiral Sir Sidney Smith, episodes 'in the nature of tapestries hung upon a solid frame of historical fact'. The solidest frame present belongs to Isabelle Laroche, the 'ripe fruit' of whose lips Lieutenant Smith first tastes in 'the sweet coolth of a West Indian twilight,' Isabelle wearing a billowing creation of pale yellow ('She was French by birth, but what of that?'). She next turns up in Normandy as la Comtesse de Guichen in flowered white mousselin, her startling *décolletage* a target for the bold kisses of Lieutenant Phélypeaux of the Engineers ('the army, you know'), while le Comte arranges go-ahead lectures on Rousseau for the domestics (it is 1783) and invites M. Danton to dine. After the 'pouting ripeness' of the Lady Ingrid Hellner in peach-coloured velvet, Captain Smith finds Isabelle again, now Citizeness Guichen and in a roomy chiffon affair, then in pale yellow gauze with gold accessories, and lastly, as a mettlesome gesture of *antisansculottisme*, sporting dark red velvet with lace ruffles.

In Constantinople, the Admiral's 'princess of the Caribbean Isles' has chosen a model of filmy black whose simplicity is relieved by a red rose 'from the Sultan's hot-houses' and the violet hollows under her eyes. The happy pair are offered *figues surprise* by an enemy, the *surprise* being a dash of prussic acid in the cream sauce. 'Delicious!' cries Sir Sidney having wisely declined sauce. Isabelle swallows a heaped spoonful and pitches headlong to the floor. Sir Sidney looks sharp with first

Christmas Reviews of Books for Girls: 1951

aid: 'There was salt on the table, and water. He wrought with Isabelle as best he could . . .'

One wonders what features historical novels of our own period will contain. Will future generations find motor bicycles, shepherd's pie, chicken coops and television irresistibly intriguing? *Humphrey the Garage-hand* may be the very thing for a bored youngster seated snugly in Dad's space-ship while the family flips over to Venus ('Oh, Mum, not Venus *again!*') for a compressed-vitamin picnic.

LATE VICTORIAN PREOCCUPATIONS

(a) AERATED WATERS

1952

'THE personal charm of the hostess counts for something even among people who are so dependent on luxury as the English upper classes,' announces Mrs. C. S. Peel in her *How to Keep House* (1897), but it is not really charm at which Mrs. Peel is aiming, it is efficiency. In her opening chapters, she deals with the best expenditure outlay for incomes ranging from £200 a year ('Holidays spent with friends') to £2,000, naturally feeling rather more at home with the latter sum. Was there, one wonders, some social *cachet* in the presence and use of aerated waters? These refreshing beverages are not mentioned until we reach the £400 bracket and then they are constantly budgeted for, sometimes ranking in importance with 'Groom-gardener, to live out', sometimes linked unsuitably with cleaning materials, flowers and soap.

Mrs. Peel is scornful of the muddled and the improvident. 'Sullenness, or even temper, on the part of the housemaid may surely be forgiven' when, having prepared herself for the afternoon (black dress, muslin apron, turn down collar, cuffs, cap), it is suddenly sprung on her that a spare room must be made ready (biscuits at the bedside and, of course, aerated waters). This lack of foresight may well have extended to other departments, enabling the affronted housemaid to have her revenge later in the day by popping a spiteful face round the door shortly before dinner and crying triumphantly, 'If you please, ma'am, we're right out of aerated waters.' Follow Mrs. Peel, spend lavishly on aerated waters, and avoid such uncomfortable moments.

Let us see how a really experienced mistress sets about the week. Sailing into the larder on Monday morning, she finds, smiling a welcome from the shelves, the remains of a forequarter of cold lamb, the carcass, two legs and one wing of a cold boiled chicken, and half a bowl of fruit salad. 'The mistress takes in the situation and disposes of the materials', 'disposes of' in the sense of decides what to do for the best with. Monday's meals more or less settle themselves, it being only necessary to order bacon (to accompany the fricassee of chicken), cream for the tomato soup, fillets of plaice (to precede the cold lamb, now making a dramatic reappearance as *croustades à la diable*), and partridges. That takes care of Monday. Tuesday's breakfast is but a snackette: omelette with green peas, cold partridge, and bacon (a butter-dish to each two covers).

Meals below stairs are chancy (not a hope of aerated waters), luncheon on September 9 being substantially the same as in the dining-room, the servants being denied nothing but Yorkshire pudding, cold partridge, and custard with their jam tart. On August 7, however, having sent aloft clear soup, fillets of plaice, tartare sauce, potatoes, veal cutlets, peas, chocolate soufflé, cheese and dessert, we find the servants' hall gazing bemused at the cold meat and pickles that Mrs. Peel has firmly prescribed for them. Was sullenness, or even temper perhaps, being punished? Is it conceivable that Agnes had once again become flummoxed over the aerated waters? Had cook forgotten to enter up the Duplicate-Order Book, or had she taken exception to a routine check of her back premises, her sinks and her grease traps? 'Should the cook resent this inspection, let her realize that it is your house and that she is yet your servant, and if she does not appreciate the position, etc., etc.'. Cold meat and pickles may well bring it home to her, and also to Agnes for not comprehending that 'at all meals, aerated waters should be in readiness'.

Cooks, it seems, come in five kinds: the cook-housekeeper, the professed cook, the cook, the plain cook, and the cook-general. Of these, the jolliest kind to be is the professed cook. Cook-housekeepers may get £10 a year more but it entails that fussing business of composing menus, peering up chimneys to detect soot, and ensuring that a *couvre-pied* is available in each spare room for warding off draughts from visitors' feet. Nobody wants to catch a chill while sipping their very own private supply of aerated waters. The professed cook, in care-free ease, can devote her time to making things agreeably hot for the others: She must 'see that the behaviour of the kitchen-maid and scullerymaid is satisfactory . . . see that what cooking is done by the under-maids is done properly'. And when surfeited with chivying, she may inspect the stores or chat with the butler (clean-shaven, except in the case of an ex-soldier, when a moustache may be retained).

Furthermore, no hour is laid down at which the professed cook must rise, while the cook is down at 6.45 a.m. and wiping the larder shelves, the plain cook is down at 6.30 a.m. and doing the dining-room grate (whilst the clouds of dust are settling, she gets busy with doorstep and brasses), and the cook-general is down at 6 a.m. and, before breakfast is so much as cleared, she has cleaned doorstep, brasses, tidied kitchen and larder 'and put on a plain pudding'. 'It is difficult', muses Mrs. Peel, reflecting on the cook-general's life, 'to define the duties of such domestics, for really they are supposed to do the entire work of the house.' Therefore, there being no parlourmaid, it is the cook-general who must, on the stroke of 10 p.m., bring in the aerated waters.

Mrs. Peel generously supplies a most varied list of helpful household hints. Parlourmaids may clean no boots other than patent boots. Soot is a valuable manure: dissuade the sweep from making off with it. The *third* sitting-room is dusted by the housemaid (at just about 6.52 a.m.). If a guest 'has had her bicycle cleaned, she should certainly remember the fact when bestowing her *douceurs*'. Remove beetles by means of the 'Demon' beetle trap, or, if your nerves are equal to it, dart after lights out 'into the room where they congregate' and lay about you with a shovel. Beetles are allergic to rhubarb leaves but regard footwear as edible and tasty. Remove flies by the simple method of seizing a damp duster and squashing them on the windows. And do remember, when shutting up the house, to smear *all* metal articles with mutton fat.

It is on the subject of drains that Mrs. Peel comes so very much into her own. Flush these every day with water, 'the sudden rush of one bucketful' being more effective than any amount of tame trickling. As for the rival claims of water-borne and earth sanitation, those interested 'should read the works on the subject from the pen of Dr. V. Poore'. If you

Late Victorian Preoccupations

favour the earth system, select your 'patent automatic seat' and do make sure that only the top spit of garden soil is used; you will need first to dry it in a shed and then riddle it; mix it with ashes, if you feel you must, but this practice will be mere embroidery. Water-borne systems are all very well, but what about the 'back pressure of foul gases'? Here, however, the servants will come in very handy, a sore throat, blood poisoning, or even typhoid below stairs being a useful reminder that the moment has come for an expert to remove the 'D' traps and cast a knowledgeable eye into the inspection chambers.

One would hardly dare to question Mrs. Peel. One just wonders at what point in the Victorian era it was *de rigueur* for the butler to 'open the drawing-room door wide and say in a loud voice, "Dinner is on the table".

(b) CYCLING ROADSTERS
1951

The bicycle, though plainly decreasingly popular, is part of everyday life. We do not now give it a thought, let alone a hostile one, but this has by no means always been so.

The Badminton Library, that invaluable encyclopaedia of healthful British Sports and Pastimes, produced its Cycling volume in 1887 and a spirited picture it gives of the advent and reception of 'the graceful piece of mechanism'. The Badminton Library was dedicated to H.R.H. The Prince of Wales and intending wheelmen, cheered by this august company, were further reassured as to the propriety of this form of locomotion by the fact that 'there is not a crowned head in Europe who has not a stud of these useful iron steeds'. A Royal princess was mounted on a Challenge tricycle. The Lord of the Thousand Elephants (son of the King of Siam) snapped up a bicycle. The Khedive of Egypt purchased several tricycles and covered them in silver plating. The highest, it was clear, were in favour of the contrivances.

The less exalted did not take to them at all. Hostility reigned and enraged rustics were for ever darting out and pushing riders into the ditch. On one startling occasion, the driver of the St. Alban's coach lashed out with his whip at a

Girls will be Girls

passing cyclist (£2 fine), while the guard threw an iron ball on a rope between the spokes, neatly upsetting the rider (£5). The police were lively with penalties for Furious Driving, cycles being carriages within the meaning of the Act. In the famous Over Turnpike case, the gatekeepers demanded a toll of five shillings from a bicyclist, subsequently 'pushing him off and detaining his lamp' (verdict for the bicyclist). As *The Times* in 1878 put it, 'the bicycle has come to the front and is fighting for its existence.'

The fight was won. Soon sober citizens were everywhere a-wheel, clergymen finding tricycles particularly useful for speedy parish work, darting now here, now there, and in reasonable safety ('even in the wildest districts of the country, the half-brick of welcome is now seldom heaved at the cycling stranger'). Innkeepers' hearts learned to leap up at the sound of wildly tinkling bells, heralding the arrival of a group of 'wandering velocipedists'. The Sociable Tricycle appeared, which provided 'the chance of inducing some adorable being of the gentler sex to share one's pilgrimage on wheels'. One never knew, however; ladies riding solo and anxious for an unmolested spin, were advised to adopt the protective camouflage of the Cyclists' Touring Club grey uniform, 'which so closely resembles that ordinarily worn by the wife of the parson or doctor that the bucolic intelligence sets down the passing stranger as probably a friend or acquaintance of the that local lady' and decides against a brick welcome. We find the year 1881 closed, as far as cycles were concerned, quietly, 'with a very lengthy discussion on the gearing of tricycles'.

The Badminton Library impresses two things on the beginner: the importance of 'artistic ankle work' and of scientific falling ('quite an art in itself'). Firstly, ankle work. 'The tyro must momentarily suppose that he has gone a few steps backward in the Darwinian line of human descent and that he is once again quadrumanous' and in this frame of mind he may then mount The Home Trainer, patented by Mr. Milbrowe Smith of West Bromwich. This ingenious device will help him to master 'the rudiments of ankle action' and to achieve eventually 'a thoroughly irreproachable ankle action', always realizing that 'an uneven ankle action is possibly worse

Eric Brought up to Date

boy, thou shouldst have learnt at thy mother's knee, if thy mother's knee had ever been anywhere but under a bridge table.

'Oh, don't just stand there gaping, Russell. Bugger off!'

The saintly youth, whose heart clave to Eric, pouted and withdrew.

'Hormones all wrong,' vouchsafed Montagu, the knowledgeable. 'I rather wonder if a change of sex isn't his answer, though I doubt if Matron is quite up to the injections. I sort of see him as a deaconess.'

Proximity to the sea ensured a plentiful fish diet for the Roslynites – cod in many palatable guises, kippers, and an occasional smelt. It was through a nutritious haze of haddock fumes that Mr. Rose, the master on duty, addressed the boys prior to grace at supper that evening.

'Attention, please. Attlay, will you kindly put down that cruet. Now, it has come to my notice that some of you juniors have been utilizing the flush-toilet in the study passage, thus seriously incommoding its rightful occupants. This detestable practice will cease forthwith and all who have been so offending are to come and report themselves to me in my lounge this evening. Benedictus benedicat. Stand up the boy who threw that roll!'

'Lounge! Toilet!' expostulated Eric. 'Where the hell does Jumbo get these ruddy second-rate ushers from?' while little Verny, egged on by the infamous Ball, and with his cherubic face alight with mischief and merriment, darted from the room and scratched ROSE IS NON-U all over the forbidden walls.

Nobody owned up to the roll-throwing, and though the comestible had appeared to come from Ball's direction, Mr. Rose had not the spirit left to accuse him though in his younger days he would have won the respect of all by hurling his bicycle-clips at the offender. But it was long, weary years since he had answered Dr. Rowlands' tempting advertisement in the *Morning Post* ('Master required to teach in recognized school. Salary') and only the knowledge of his high calling and the need to eat had sustained him through his struggle with headstrong youth.

Labour on, Walter Rose! Labour on, though the soil seem barren and the seed sterile. On, Walter, on! There's a pension, meagre though it be, at the end of it.

As Eric was leaving the dining-room, a loving hand was placed on his shoulder.

'Eric, dear Eric!'

Girls will be Girls

'Oh, for God's sake stop pawing me about, Russell. What is it now?'

'Oh, Eric, Eric, I grieve for you.'

'Mind your own blasted business.'

'To see you thus, careless of your brother's welfare! Where, where is the mould of stainless honour in which I thought you cast? And though I grieve, there is one who grieves even more,' said Edwin, pointing reverently upwards.

'What? *Mr. Harley?* You must be mad,' riposted Eric, the astrophysics master being known to inhabit poky quarters on the floor above.

'No, no, no! You deliberately misunderstand me.'

'Oh, put a sock in it, you little wet!'

Stung, and sad beyond measure or telling at the ill-merited retort, Russell, a keen marine biologist, flung from the room and out through the Faraday Memorial Gates and down on to the shore. His ears dulled by the mingled scream of weltering tempest and plangent wave, he stood for a space admiring the translucent pools, the audacious crabs. Anemones were the devout boy's special interest and he seemed never to tire of watching the crimson sea-flowers waving their long tentacula. Recking little of the water that squelched its way into his ankle supports, Edwin set off briskly in quest of a white plumosa for little Verny's treasured collection. And the holy lad fully forgave in his heart all Eric's coldness.

It is well that he did! It is well, indeed! Come back, Edwin Russell, come back! The sea is rising, boy, and that way disaster lies. Come back, I say again! Does he hear? No, alas, he does not. He squelches on.

'Eric, dear, you're looking a bit off colour.' Thus Mrs. Rowlands, in roomy rust-hued slacks, encountering Eric outside the seniors' telly room.

'Oh, I'm O.K. thanks, Mrs. Rowlands.'

'Let it be Sybil, dear, *please!*'

Eric flushed with pleasure.

'I haven't seen anything of you for ages, dear. You've been quite neglecting me. And Jumbo's off again tomorrow.' She sighed and toyed for a moment with the giant cairngorm at her breast. 'Do come along for a chat some afternoon, and I'll give you anchovy toast, and tea, and – er – sympathy.'

Now, Eric, now or never! This is it, lad! Speak out! Tell her that you don't care all that much about anchovy toast.

Late Victorian Preoccupations

than no ankle action at all'. And now for scientific falling. 'Falling forwards from a bicycle is by no means a difficult exploit. The peculiar form of tumble that ensues is known by the distinctive name of "the cropper", or "Imperial Crowner".' Protect your hands with a stout pair of gloves and fall, where possible, on to the road, which will produce 'a series of somersaults, nothing like so serious in its results as a dead stop against a wall'. Do try not to fall on cinders ('very disfiguring'), which may leave your face as though tattooed in blue streaks. Should this occur, instantly clap on large linseed-meal poultices and entrust your 'disintegrated membranes' to Mother Nature. Having fallen successfully on to the road, and completed your series of somersaults, you should, 'after the first pain has gone off, essay to move'. Don't just lie there.

As to clothing, an all-wool programme is advised (ladies taking advantage of the popular all-wool corset). Overlook nothing: 'a sore throat is often to be traced to the linen band round the neck of a flannel shirt.' Here are the essentials— 'a medium thickness combination, a lounging shirt of light cashmere and a stocking cap of knitted material. Should the tourist entertain the slightest suspicion of the dryness of his sheets, he can obviate cold in the head or worse dangers by sleeping in his cap.' For couples mounted upon Sociables, the Norfolk Jacket is recommended, and 'riders with abnormal calves will do well to tone them down with wide and somewhat baggy knickerbockers'. Beware of 'the hard and unyielding garter' (varicose veins), of double seating for cloth breeches (blisters), of undetachable washleather seats (rucks and folds galore).

Beware of much else besides: of cramp in the toe-joints, of putting your foot amongst the spokes, of 'that most dangerous accident, a blow behind the heel on the tendon Achilles' (females on Sociables should make sure that their pedals are fitted with the Cheylesmore clutch). Always carry 'a combination gong' among your spares ('nothing can be more annoying on a dark night than the loss of the clapper of the bell').

Fully equipped, with your ankle action all that it should

Girls will be Girls

be, your solid rubber tyres snugly fitted to your outer semi-lunes, your C.T.C. silver badge ('a passport to cheery kindness'), several hours of practice road-falling behind you and your conviction that 'in mud which exceeds three inches, you must get off and walk', you are ready for a tour. If lonely, advertise in the *C.T.C. Gazette* 'asking for a consort'. State your social position, so that nobody feels uncomfortable. It may well lead to a 'hearty friendship', the swopping of two bicycles for a Sociable, and hours of happy wheeling together down Life's Cinder-free Track.

CHRISTMAS REVIEWS OF BOOKS FOR GIRLS

1954

CHEERYBUZZFUZZ

The School on the Precipice. By Nancy Moss (Chambers).
Fourth Form Detectives. By Nancy Breary (Blackie).
One Day Event. By Josephine Pullein-Thompson (Collins).

W ELCOME, thrice welcome to Nancy Moss, a newcomer in the finest Brazil tradition. This is the real thing.

The school in question, Cliff House (headmistress Miss Pusey. Colours: maroon-and-cream), is somewhat riskily situated: 'the last fall of cliff took an acre or so of ground down with it,' and indeed the major portion of the hockey field now forms part of the foreshore, forcing the school hockey aces, Irene Fletcher and Maud Draper, to join the local Ladies' Club ('There's television in the club-house, I've been told'). However, on the limited remaining terrain, a great deal happens. Susan Savage diverts from the cliff top a runaway horse bearing the head girl, Beryl Marston ('I won't try to thank you, dear'), and subsequently receives the Marston Award for Heroism, which turns out to be a brooch 'intrinsically valuable, being made of solid hall-marked silver and studded with a fine diamond', the *ensemble* being in the form of a rearing horse.

The headmistress has a barely satisfactory brother who drives the school shooting-brake down a disused tunnel as a preparatory move to dynamiting the school buildings and collecting the insurance money. This novel plot is foiled by Beryl Marston herself, who unselfishly misses the Rambling Club ramble to achieve it, and is witnessed by Susan Savage through Elsa Marling-Brown's telescope. There is the school wag, Cissie Carew ('Cissie was a tonic'), who is given to saying 'Cheerybuzzfuzz' and 'Bung-ho', and who sings the solo part in *The Ballad of the Singing Sands* ('That child has the voice of an angel') at the Kent County Festival, Miss Lonsdale being quite beside herself 'at the excellent quality of the vocal material under her baton'. Then Susan wakes one morning to find that during the night her pigtails have been cut off ('Her face flushed with anger'), and Cissie, who is responsible, treats herself to a perm at Maison Raoul's. There is also a Fast Set who smoke scented cigarettes: 'you'll find them useful as a screen when you're nervous'.

The book contains a daring innovation. A needle match against a visiting team is not concerned with either cricket or net-ball:

> 'Check!' said the Cudham College girl. Ada Mackintosh gazed long and earnestly at the board, but she had no choice. There was only one move open to her. She made it. 'Check!' said the Cudham College girl, inexorably again. Almost despairingly, Ada glared at the board.

In *Fourth Form Detectives* we are at Merrilees Manor (head-mistress: Miss Petrie. Colours: brown-and-scarlet), with girls called Loveday Scott, Rosemary Heathcote and Natalie Tottenham. The head girl is Gretchen Halstead ('her people are the Hampshire Halsteads, you know, and they have a glorious place in the New Forest'). Gretchen Halstead is also 'considered a cert for County hockey next year'. There is pleasantly varied activity, with the Posture Competition to decide on the best ladies-in-waiting for the Pageant (Prologue spoken by Gretchen Halstead. Epilogue spoken by Gretchen Halstead), the upsetting by Wanda Tottenham of Jill's violet toilet water, and the day when Gretchen Halstead invites Jill to bowl to her ('Send me along a few balls, will you?'). After a false report of damage to an exhibition *gouache* ('Still Life', by Gretchen Halstead), Jill is discovered to have remarkable ventriloquial powers (' "Your voice is really very funny," Gretchen Halstead encouraged') and plays Puck in the Pageant ('Jill was an absolute hoot, she really was').

'June hasn't turned up yet,' says a character in *One Day Event*, 'but I think I hear her hoofs,' thus setting the tone for

Christmas Reviews of Books for Girls: 1954 and 1955

what follows. This is the ideal book for pony-maniacs as, when doubts and difficulties arise, there is always Major Holbrooke to make everything clear:

> In other words, his head, neck and inside shoulder will be bent to the inside, his inside foreleg will be off the school track, his inside hindleg will follow in the track of the outside foreleg and his outside hindleg follows a track of its own. The horse's head is flexed in the opposite direction to the movement.

Got it? Better to make quite sure for we are in the world of Mrs. Van Cutler (a novice judge), Susan Barington-Brown, Merry Hemlock-Jones, Maureen Painter, Mrs. Cresswell (of 'Dormers') and Mrs. Exeter, in a fashionable shade of carbon grey, who is getting on in years and 'finds herself landed with masses of half-broken Anglo-Arabs'. The Exeters aren't, alas, dressage-minded but there are lots of things to take the mind off this sad lapse: mucking out Spartan and Echo, for instance, or undoing the stud billets of your double bridle, or getting yet another canister of hoof oil, or saying 'I do so want a lovely dressage seat' or 'A dropped noseband will prevent evasions'. After a good bit of lunging, June Cresswell announces that 'everyone knows that too early use of the double bridle spoils the development of the horse's cadence'. Well, I knew it, of course, and I'm sure you did too, but . . . *everyone*?

CHRISTMAS REVIEWS OF BOOKS FOR GIRLS

1955

PHOOO-OOO-OOF!

Kemlo and the Star Men. By E. C. Eliott (Nelson).
Mission to Mars. By Patrick Moore (Burke).
Susan's Stormy Term. By Nancy Moss (Chambers).

A swiftish glance at this year's books for young persons

shows that Space has triumphed in popularity over Ponies, and in *Kemlo and the Star Men* we find ourselves on Satellite Belt K (motto: Pause and Ponder), complete with space-born inhabitants, games-room, and a resident band in the concert hall. Kemlo takes the juvenile Krillie (voice just broken) on the Space Scouts' sky patrol: speed, 28,000 m.p.h. Before zooming down the ramp and through the exit chute, Kemlo waits, naturally, until the magnetized gravity ray is being fed through the launching base. Then he ejects his stabilisers (well, wouldn't you?) and feeds the powerful holding rays in a cloudy veil round the craft; conversation, however, remains entirely earthy ('Don't be daft!'). Landing on a star gives Krillie a 'fluttery feeling in his tummy', for which Kemlo reprimands him ('You're cross with me'). They collect a handful of unlovely organisms ('Brrr!') for the specimen box, and the atmosphere is eerie: 'I'm beginning to wish I were back in my cubicle reading Shakespeare. The Bard has a word for everything.' Yes, indeed. Suddenly, an elaborate orange saucer twirls into view, lands, opens its sliding doors and lowers its ramp. For a time we too pause and ponder. What will appear ('S'pose it's—*things*!)? Egg-shaped Martian robots lumber out ('Ooooh —look!') and a radiotronic report is made to Satellite K ('Is the Duty Officer there, please?'). An extra large robot teeters forth ('Ooh—isn't he big!') and is inclined to wave his antennae and make trouble, but all is set to rights, fruit juice is swigged, the Balbo Emrich rescue team shows up, and the Chief Elder ('awesome') creates a number of honorary Star Men. Personally, I'm staying right here in dear old Melton Mowbray.

Compared with all this, *Mission to Mars* is like a simple bicycle outing to Croydon. Slimly built sixteen-year-old Maurice Gray arrives in Woomera to find Sir Robert Lanner ('ice-cold eyes') and Dr. Mellor ('vice-like grip'), but not his uncle, Professor Yorke, who is stranded on Mars with a buckled rocket ('Phoof!'). Volunteers attempt a rescue ('Blast-off's timed for 7.30. Feel nervy?'). Maurice conks out at blast-off ('Did I let you down?') but is soon sitting up and spluttering 'Ph-oof!'. Then he clambers into magnetic boots and nips outside to rectify the distance register, jammed at blast-off ('Phoof!'). Bruce, negligent about his space suit motor,

Christmas Reviews of Books for Girls: 1954 and 1955

floats off and Maurice saves him ('a pretty good show'), faints, comes to, and smartly records another 'Phoof!'. Nearing Mars, Maurice dozes off ('Phoof! I was dead away, and no mistake'), the rocket bursts through the Violet Layer, which is disappointingly not a stratum of especially scrumptious chocs, and makes a heavy landing on a reddish-ochre plain ('Ph-oof!'). Nothing very much happens and there are no Martians ('It's rather a pity but there it is'). There is a dust-storm ('Poof! I didn't bargain for this'), a tiring walk ('Phoof!'), quicksands (yes, 'Poof!'), a largish animal with red hair and scales ('This will give our biologists a shock, and no mistake'), and a huge bat with green eyes ('Whoa, Horace!'). The stranded scientists are found and Maurice phoofs his way back through the Violet Layer. Prior to this jaunt, there has been, in 1966, a landing on the Moon: 'the whole thing went without a hitch from start to finish'. Phoo-ooo-oof!

Devotees of schoolgirl literature may care to attempt a context of the following stirring passage:

> Her arm, which Irene had gripped, was dropped as if it had become suddenly red-hot. There was a deadly silence. Then Irene spoke. Her voice was thick.
> 'Are you daring to accuse the head girl of the school?'
> Susan was pale and her lips quivered slightly, but she spoke without faltering.
> 'Yes, I am, because I saw what you did. So did my friends.'
> 'How dare you?' breathed out Irene, passionate with anger. *'How dare you!'*

Well? Middle-period Brazil, you think? Vintage Winifred Darch? Dorita Fairlie Bruce? Early May Wynne? It is none of these delightful things but current Nancy Moss who, with *Susan's Stormy Term*, strengthens the splendid impression she made last year with *The School on the Precipice*.

We are still precipitous and Irene Fletcher is indeed head girl but skilfully doubles it with leadership of the Black Sheep society (associate members: Annette Ledoux, Felicity Ulston, Monica Martineau). Their desperate aim is to 'put the kybosh on Maud Draper and her precious hockey team'. Trouncing other teams might lead to compulsory games, and then 'we

Girls will be Girls

shouldn't have the chance of doing the exciting things we've all got planned for the spring'. So Irene keeps key players in detention and Felicity removes the brake-blocks from Bertha Marston's bicycle, the outside right having an unenviable ride down Corkscrew Hill (1 in 3). Horrid things go on in attics:

> 'Well, this is my answer – look!' With a fierce, brutal movement, she lifted Bertha bodily up by the strap and swung her to the window. She was a very strongly built girl and she moved Bertha almost effortlessly.

However, in the end, hockey is firmly established (centre-forward: Elsie Gordon), and there's more chess, with Susan Savage playing a dashing game at fifth board. Pleasures come thick and fast—walks ('The downs look swish for a ramble.'), a fire-alarm ('The girls rushed headlong for the exits'), the Headmistress's unfortunate brother ('He's up to some mischief in that cave, I'll be bound'), Madame Raoul's hair-dos ('very charming and a real artist'), girls called Mavis Moorhead, Alerdyce Bell, Cora Wimbore and Lola Consett, and there's a skewbald quadruped which 'lips interestedly' at Susan's gym tunic ('He's only saying how-d'you-do').

CRITIC'S CORNER: GENTLEMEN

MON MOT!

Ma Vie. By Serge Lifar, translated by James Holman Mason (Hutchinson, 1970).

> Oh the urge to see Serge,
> What a thrill, what a pill,
> What a purge!

sang the crazed balletomanes in a pre-war Farjeon revue. Well, they can see him again now, and not plain but tuppence-coloured, in an autobiography that is as hilarious as any I can remember. The translator has finely caught the spirit of the thing and has come across with gem after gem. Diaghilev sends a parcel ('What could it be? Some knick-knacks?'). Diaghilev becomes chummy ('Our two souls met together in an upsurge towards the Beautiful'). Lifar becomes practical ('I shook off my musings').

About his abilities as a dancer, the Paris-based Russian is not in any way *shy*. Tributes flow ('Bravo, Lifar') and Diaghilev is pleased ('Thank you, Lifar'). Lifar criticises Pavlova for being unenterprising ('It's possible, Lifar'), takes over the choreography of *Prométhée* ('Upon my word, Lifar'), and a tiff follows ('Calm down, Lifar').

The excitement quickens with the end of the phoney war and old Gerry's occupation of the capital ('Bravo, Lifar. . . . Thank you, Lifar. . . . You must stay, Lifar'). Officially mobilized, he is given a job as observer on the Eiffel Tower (forbidden to use the lift). There follow several near-shaves from assassination. In *Spectre de la Rose*, a sword flashed ('I avoided the blade'), and a French submarine which he should have boarded (prevented by a heavy chest cold) plunged straight to the bottom. The Resistance plans an abduction by both 'hydroplane' and *wagon-lit*, but fails ('a hitch in their arrangements'). Trains blow up, aeroplanes are chased by the devilish English, Balinese dancers seek his blood. Stalin desperately parachutes in an agent to shoot Lifar ('He opened his rain-coat and showed me his weapon'), opera singers aim pistols, in New York they threaten to blow up the theatre ('Look out, Lifar'), and in Australia Mr. Menzies obligingly acts as bodyguard. But the elusive Pimpernel wins through and when, during a ballet, a heavy scenic counterweight, aimed at Lifar, crashes down, we find that he has been inspired to 'change the variations', hooray hooray, and it misses him. Well, hooray, anyway.

FAT OWL REMOVED

Bunter's Last Fling. By Frank Richards (Cassell, 1965).
Greyfriars School. A Prospectus. By J. S. Butcher (Cassell, 1965).

At long last it is the end of the road for the monstrous Billy Bunter, the revolting, chortling fatty in the tightest trousers in Greyfriars and the permanently straitened circumstances, despite a rich stockbroker pater resident at Bunter Villa, Reigate. Obese and, one suspects, impotent, he is like no schoolboy that ever was and seems in character and person to have more in common with a gin-swilling, petty-cash-fiddling, perspiring middle-aged businessman, endlessly swapping dirty stories with the lads and chatting up Miss Loosely in the snug.

The Greyfriars stories appeared originally in *The Magnet* (defunct by 1940) and generally speaking were never read by public schoolboys. They were in a different class, in two senses, from the *Boy's Own Paper* and *The Captain* and would have been considered ludicrously false and feeble. To their gullible juvenile readers they gave a markedly unreal picture of public schools and did a hearty disservice both to fact and to fiction. The wearisome repetitions, the implausibility, the tastelessness, the Ho! Ho! Ho! and Ha! Ha! Ha! are over. To borrow a phrase, He! He! He!

Critic's Corner: Gentlemen

Bunter's creator, Charles Hamilton (alias Frank Richards and many other names), was a charming and courteous robot writer and what author with a life to live would blame him for mercilessly milking such a profitable subject? The final story, *Bunter's Last Fling*, reveals on the jacket a coloured likeness of the Fat Owl of the Remove greedily stuffing in a farewell cream horn, gig-lamps gleaming. The story begins with the words 'Oh, crikey!' Enough.

Mr. J. S. Butcher, an ardent Bunterphile, has now produced a Prospectus of Greyfriars School, and the many admirers of the deplorable dumpling will pounce with glee (the style is catching) on this, the only published guide to the school. It covers every aspect of the varied activities, with comprehensive plans of the buildings and grounds (too generously wooded for a headmaster's peace of mind). The fun here, and it is considerable, lies in the aping of the real thing. One well knows the brave struggles of lowish-grade scholastic establishments to bump up their charms.

> The old laundry has now been skilfully converted into a self-service dining-room for Cromwell House (Mr. J. B. F. Dicey. Colours: puce and buff). Juniors wait on Prefects, and vice versa. All boys take a turn in the kitchen and at the character-building sink.

A FINE FRENZY

No Poets' Corner in the Abbey. By David Phillips (Duckworth, 1971).

There has often been an affectionate place in human hearts for the supremely bad. Think of the wobbly operatic arias of Florence Foster Jenkins. Think of the merry improbabilities of *Young England*. Think of the Albert Memorial. Think too, of the uninhibited and free-flowing verse of William McGonagall:

Girls will be Girls

> As I chanced to see trouts leaping in the River o' Glenshee,
> It helped to fill my heart with glee,
> And to anglers I would say without any doubt
> There's plenty of trouts there for pulling out.

McGonagall was living quietly as a weaver in Dundee when suddenly in 1877 the Poetic Muse descended without warning upon him. He was 52 and out the delightful poems effortlessly flowed. Anxious to share these unexpected gifts with Her Majesty, he at once set out on foot for Balmoral (the sole reception, from a lodgekeeper, was outstandingly frosty). He found that disasters sparked him off best of all—the collapse of the Tay Bridge, a good famine somewhere, floods in China, a ferry boat fatality, a theatre fire in Exeter, and away he went:

> And in the spectators' faces were depicted fear and consternation;
> While the news flew like lightning to the Fire Brigade station.

His poems appeared regularly in the *Weekly News* but, keen to meet his public face to face, he rented halls (COME EARLY AND BRING SIXPENCE) and, rigged out in Rob Roy tartan and with his pince-nez carefully adjusted, he would let fly, waving a sword during 'Bruce at Bannockburn', the front rows prudently ducking during the more fiery passages. He varied these recitals with performances of *Macbeth* (twice nightly) in an arresting costume covered with glittering silver spangles, fully reported by the critic of the *Journal*:

> McGonagall as Macbeth refused to die when run through by Macduff; he maintained his feet and flourished his weapon about the ears of his adversary in such a way that there was an apparent probability of a real tragedy. Macduff, continually telling him to go down, became at length so incensed that he gave him a smart rap over the fingers with the flat of his sword. McGonagall dropped his weapon but dodged and pranced as if to wrestle.

And eventually the only way of silencing the kipper-coloured and slightly cracked tragedian was to trip him ignominiously up.

Poor fish-eyed and permanently insolvent McGonagall became speedily a public joke (but not to kind David Phillips). He was set upon in the streets, where he struck gamely out at rowdies with his umbrella, and at his performances he found himself on the receiving end of cornucopias of decaying fruit and bad eggs. He remained totally undiscouraged and we need not be sorry for him. He had no sense of humour and, unless they actually threw things, any noise that an audience made was in his ears a triumphant ovation. His belief in his genius never wavered. And rightly. After all, we read him still.

BLOOMINGS

One Life. By Christiaan Barnard and Curtis Bill Pepper (Harrap, 1970).

'Everything's coming up roses' Ethel Merman used to sing in *Gypsy*. How delightful can be these unexpected comings up and bloomings. It seems only yesterday that everything in London's garden suddenly started coming up Lord Goodman (a prolific floribunda of great charm and fragrance). And recently everything's been coming up Professor Barnard, the bouncy heart-transplanter, freshly bewifed and with those impressive molars a-gleam. A sturdy rambler, would you say? A hardy climber? His book, alas, reminds one less of a rose than of a Cape gooseberry.

An autobiography written by two persons hardly inspires confidence. Who provided what? Presumably the Professor and his hospital records made with the facts while Curtis Bill Pepper tidied it all up and fed in the mush. The aim is clear enough: to provide a generous hunk of medical history dolled up in dramatic form (there are endless chunks of what can only be invented dialogue) and then serve it out to the vast public that has already whetted its morbid appetite for doctors and illness with *Emergency Ward Ten, Dr. Kildare,* the B.B.C.'s *The Doctors,* and those dear hoot-tooters up in Tannochbrae.

This treatment of history is a pity, for the facts themselves are of absorbing interest and, though the percentage of subsequent deaths is daunting, the achievement is considerable and the Professor's pertinacity and cleverness are remarkable.

Girls will be Girls

However, he and Curtis Bill Pepper can sob all the way to the bank as nothing can stop the book from, as they say, heading the charts. In a startling passage, we find the first transplant patient, Louis Washkansky, awaiting a new heart from the unconscious donor, a girl dying after a street accident. The Professor finds time to ponder (and to cheer up any reader who may be suffering from doubts):

> 'You know,' I said, 'I would die a wonderful death if I could feel that as a result of my death somebody else would be able to live. It's better than just dying for your country or your flag, no?' 'Maybe,' said Sister Papendieck, who was on her knees under the bed, reading the urine output. Christ on the Cross would have done it, too. If there had been a possibility of doing a transplant, of using one of His organs, He would have given it immediately . . . He worried about the criminals next to Him, about their suffering and death. If He could have given His heart and kidneys to save either of them, He would have done that, too.

And He might possibly add to His donations by giving Professor Barnard a piece of His mind.

OLD PARTY

A Case of Human Bondage. By Beverley Nichols (Secker & Warburg, 1966).

For the first and only time, poor Mr. Maugham has become a gusher. Sludge flows ceaselessly out concerning his amatory misfortunes. Garden-loving Beverley Nichols, conquering late in life his squeamishness about things found under stones, has now added his sad little pile to the general muck-heap. One hears that the film rights have been snapped up. It now only needs a musical based on the life of Gerald Haxton (*Up From Somerset*) to round off the whole exaggerated business. The subject of Mr. Nichols's spiteful, gossipy pages would have been particularly repelled by the style in which they are written. But we must, it seems, forgive Mr. Nichols. His book has a noble purpose, 'the refutation of a libel upon a dead woman', Syrie Maugham. May one ask to which charity the handsome financial proceeds of this crusade are to go?

Boys of the King's School, Canterbury, lingering near the lawn beneath which the mortal remains of their famous old boy are doubtless revolving at a brisk pace in their casket, may be able, bending low and listening carefully, to catch a phrase or two from down below:

> I have a notion that when an old party dies it is as well to let him be. I am aware that certain persons have been preparing their recollections of me and that, anxious to publish, they have faced my death with fortitude. I can but think that the recollections are disobliging. Flattery does not sell. I do not blame them. It is not in me to judge my fellows; I am content to observe them. I am not a vindictive man and it merely amuses me to reflect that my stories will still be read when these persons and what they have thought fit to say are long since forgotten. They are small fry.

UGH MEIN PAPA!

Father Figure. By Beverley Nichols (Heinemann, 1972).

Writers' fathers have, from Dickens on, been mostly very far from satisfactory. Take Mr. Barrett, the humourless tyrant of Wimpole Street. Think of Sir George Sitwell, the egomaniac eccentric. Ponder on Godfrey Winn's Dad, who absented himself from home and espoused different interests.

Hitherto the first prize for awfulness has gone to unsaintly Dean Worsley (the dog-collar just tipped the scale) and now here is Beverley Nichols with a very strong contestant. But there is a difference. The other naughty fellows were described by their offspring with some sort of understanding, and sometimes an amused affection. Mr. Nichols writes with nothing but hatred, scorn and venom.

The book's theme is announced in the opening sentence. 'The first time I remember my father he was lying dead drunk

Girls will be Girls

on the dining-room floor.' From then on, the book is a kind of Child's Guide to Dipsomania. This Bristol solicitor of great promise had done well enough to retire in his thirties to the respectability and palm-trees of Torquay where he solaced himself with whisky and devoted his days to being as awkward as possible.

> No human brain that I have ever encountered in fiction, and certainly none in life, was so regularly and so passionately employed, over so long a period, in the exclusive labour of making others unhappy.

The tipsy sixteen-stone Philistine with the rimless, cordless eyeglass and the moustache anointed with *Pommade Hongroise*, makes a displeasing picture, either when abusing his wife or stoning dogs or buying bogus ancestral portraits. He was revoltingly maudlin in repentance, and even nastier when weaving his boozy way back to the decanter. He had a brisk manner of dealing with literature of which he disapproved: Oscar Wilde, for instance:

> My father opened the book very slowly, cleared his throat, and spat on the title page . . . Then with a swift animal gesture, he lifted the book to his mouth, closed his teeth over some of the pages, and began tearing them to shreds.

His son made three spirited attempts to do away with him. First by lacing his soup with aspirins, purchased secretly on a lightning bicycle dash to Newton Abbot. When this Borgia tactic miscarried, he released a heavy garden roller on to his father's drunken and recumbent form. And finally, and much later in life, in that *Down the Garden Path* dream cottage, he filled him up with sleeping pills which were to combine lethally with the whisky, dragged him outside into the snow and entangled him in a rose-bush. An hour passed and then the Torquay Rasputin crashed back in, hardly at all the worse for wear.

The beautiful and charming Mrs. Nichols left a will which wisely excluded him but she continued to love her sodden consort to the end of her days, loyally urging her children never to think unkindly of him ('It is not *him*', was her way of explaining the endless upsets, 'it is a disease'). She was hardly cold in her grave before her sporty husband was contemplating a more temporary attachment with some busty and cuddlesome barmaid.

It is all very well done. Mr. Nichols has never written better and his sorry tale has a dreadful fascination. But this is the second book in which he has unwisely remembered, and so late in the day, too much for comfort. Writers, however unhappy and obsessed, should not get things quite so obviously off their chests. Old men should forget. One can respect silence.

MUMBO-JUMBO AT MOUNT ARARAT

Montague Summers. By Joseph Jerome (Cecil & Amelia Woolf, 1966).

The published photograph of Montague Summers unfortunately gives him the look of a somewhat suspect Widow Twankey, sporting false curls and a centre parting and about to go on stage ('Drat that boy of mine!') and split every side in the house. Or, if not the Peking *blanchisseuse*, then some doubtful menial applying for a situation and well aware that her references contain imperfections. They did indeed. Mists decently, perhaps, now obscure much that might have made all plain. The hair was genuine but what else was? Was he a priest or wasn't he and, if so, in which camp? Whence came his doctorate? How Black were his Masses? How near a thing was the court case for you-know-what in a Bristol suburb? It is not without interest that he preferred to walk in the gutter.

He was rum and rather sinister and, quaintly dressed in shovel hat and flowing cape and buckled shoes, he made himself a *chose vue*. He burnt joss-sticks and wore purple silk socks in Lent and after taking a sparkling fourth in theology at Oxford he became an occasional schoolmaster. He added on

Girls will be Girls

two Christian names, Alphonsus Joseph-Mary. Nothing could be ordinary; even his friends tended to be called Hartwell de la Garde Grissell and Baron Jacques d'Adelswaerd Fersen. He said Mass in his private oratory at 4 Mount Ararat Road, Richmond, helped by a pallid, sickly secretary, Hector Stuart-Forbes, whom he introduced as 'my adopted son, the great musician'.

Subsequent occupiers of 4 Mount Ararat Road, took a wise step. They had it thoroughly exorcised by the parish priest.

TALLY-HO!

People and Places. By Malcolm MacDonald (Collins, 1969).

Mr. MacDonald describes his book as 'random reminiscences . . . unimportant and light-hearted' and, aiming perhaps at joviality, makes use of a weird vocabulary. No simple word will do. A horse is a trusty steed, a face is a visage or countenance, legs are nether limbs, to sleep is to slumber, a room is a chamber, the sea is the briny, a girl is a damsel, and Japan is the Land of the Cherry Blossom.

It is also, alas, the Land of the Ichiriki Tea-house, complete with simpering geishas and dancing girls called Little Peach and The Dewdrop Under the Pine Trees. Several of these Mr. MacDonald teaches how to play Blind Man's Buff ('high-pitched giggles') and, back at the hotel, how to work the lift ('screams and laughter'): *twelve* ascents are made, with Little Peach at the controls. Remembering them years later ('Each one presented me with her photograph and decorative visiting card'), he is glad that for him they will always remain 'vivacious, adorable, immortal children'. To illustrate this, and with almost inconceivable bad taste and misapplication, he quotes (and misquotes) Binyon's 'For the Fallen'—'They shall grow not old'.

After this one expects anything, and it is not long in coming. There is riding in Peking:

Critic's Corner: Gentlemen

I waved with jocular glee to the Lampson family as I sped past them. The Minister shouted 'Tally-ho!' and gave chase with fervent gusto.

There is a visit with Dorothy Dickson to Beatrice Lillie's house (' "Come in, you belated revellers" '), from where he has to telephone to Neville Chamberlain:

> Then, while I listened intently . . . I felt a pair of arms insinuate themselves across my shoulders, fold themselves round my neck, and hug me tight. Bea's voice murmured 'I think you're an excellent Secretary of State. Tell the Prime Minister so from me.' Her tone was exaggeratedly roguish in a play-acting sort of way . . . After a few moments, Bea observed in a stage whisper, 'Oh, you're so calm and sage!' I turned my head, smiled at her, and held an upraised finger against my lips to enjoin silence. She chortled mischievously and said 'Tell the Prime Minister I think you're a poppet.'

After Chamberlain's return from Munich, the High Commissioners are summoned:

> When they came through the doorway I welcomed them by turning several cartwheels across the floor and clapping my heels in the air at every convolution. They somehow gathered that this meant Chamberlain had succeeded in achieving an agreement at Munich which averted war, for I heard them laughing in a gleeful explosive way.

Casals gets a similar treat in Singapore:

> I stood on my hands and proceeded to walk upside-down along the street. At its further end I turned round and strolled back, still topsy-turvy on my hands. Casals was very pleased, and kept crying loud exclamations of surprise.

He was also foolish enough to shout 'Encore!' Later, Pandit Nehru attempts to steal the limelight with some eyeball-rolling Yogi exercises but he hasn't a chance: 'I stood on my hands, and walked round him half a dozen times', while Lady Mountbatten looked on. We look on too, saddened to see a pleasant and distinguished public figure allowed to make quite such a donkey of himself in print. What are publishers for but to raise fingers to enjoin non-publication?

Girls will be Girls
BOOTS BOOTS

Memoirs of an Academic Old Contemptible. By Donald Portway (Leo Cooper, 1971).

For this militarily-inclined book, some reliance has been placed on diaries. They provide chancy material for a writer, a verbal total recall unsifted by time and the mind. They come in two kinds. The less acceptable is the diary written to be read and, later, published:

> Dined sybaritically with Adrian, looking methought increasingly like the central figure in Fra Belli's unimaginably *réussi* triptych in the Diabolo Museum in Verona. Much good talk while we discussed a chilled Tuscan Irredenta, every grape dawn-gathered on that blessed South-Western slope high above the tawny roofs of Verismelli.

The second sort are the plainly factual ones, sometimes written so long ago and far away that age alone confers on them a kind of interest:

> Crowd restless but felt too exhausted to calm them with another miracle. Trudged to Capernaum, Barnabas very boring about some girl in Ramoth-Gilead. No rain and fig harvest disappointingly meagre. Tore new white raiment on thornbush and got very cross. Supper cold roast camel (again!). Finally turned in in filthy goat shed, v browned off and fed up.

Reading the life story of the genial, octogenarian, cold-bath-loving Colonel Portway, ex-Master of St. Catherine's College, Cambridge, who boxed four times against Oxford and has a record of twelve years whole-time service in the Royal Engineers in two wars, one wonders how far he will get before quoting *mens sana in corpore sano* and there, on page 50, up the dread words pop. Never mind. Rowing, fisticuffing, bicycling, lusty singing in Chapel, backed up by (one would conjecture) not too much disturbing thought, have combined to give him a happy and useful life, happy often in the most rum circumstances:

Critic's Corner: Gentlemen

> I thoroughly enjoyed the summer and autumn of 1915 . . . The neighbouring church was hit by an incendiary shell and was a wonderful sight as the burning spire fell to the ground . . . I was looking forward to the winter of 1915–16 with the 6th Division.

And then there were the chucklesome jokes ('The Latin for Six Mile Bottom is *Ars Longa*') and the merry riddles: 'If bread is the staff of life, what is the life of the staff? Answer: One long loaf.'

Recalled to the colours for the second conflict, it was sad to find the fireworks not always up to scratch:

> On 10 May 1940 the Bailleul gasworks went up in flames. Since then I have seen two gasworks in the UK being bombed. It is a disappointing sight – no explosion of any sort but a huge almost colourless flame . . . Plymouth was a wonderful sight when being bombed, with the searchlights all over the place, but a lot of damage was being done.

Yes: it was.

It is extremely easy to get ratty with Colonel Portway. 'The dustman . . . can hardly require a general education beyond 15 years of age' is an odious and stupid statement. When he dealt with admissions to Cambridge, 'one could usually count that a boy who was good at games would turn out fairly well' (and he is not too happy about 'high-brow intellectuals'). And after the University? 'Many young men grow up nowadays without any direct experience of adversity, one of the best means of building up a mature personality.' Like whose, for instance? Depressing that such a long and largely academic life should apparently have taught him so little of value.

RUM BABA

Baba. By Arnold Schulman (Macmillan, 1972).

Baba, the South Indian miracle-worker with 'a following of millions' was, at 46, an arresting spectacle:

Girls will be Girls

  Baba wore a bright orange dress that hung loosely down to his chunky bare feet; but the first thing one noticed was his Afro-electric hair standing straight out from all parts of his head like a black, kinky halo five or six inches wide.

Arnold Schulman, an American film script-writer, became fascinated by the thought of this delightful golliwog and set out to visit him, prudently limbering up before departure with a few meditation exercises (holding the lotus position for hours at a time) and laying in a stock of heat-resistant chocolate. Hovering in Baba's background is the good Dr. Gokok ('his thick horn-rimmed glasses made him resemble a giant, lumbering, benevolent owl'). Dr. Gokok warmly welcomes Mr. Schulman and promises a Baba audience. Dr. Gokok talks of Baba and Dr. Gokok springs a surprise:

  'Baba is an avatar,' Gokok said. 'An incarnation of God, you know. He said so.'

There now! Baba can materialize vibuthi (holy ashes) in rather over-generous quantities (a little go a long way), along with towels, rings and sweetmeats, but is a pinch too inclined to materialize 'aluminium photographs' of Baba.

Dr. Gokok's arrangements fall through and Baba proves elusive. He is able, it seems, to leave his body behind and travel through astral space and time, though when travelling *with* his body he wisely employs 'Raj Reddy, the son of a maharaja, who is Baba's personal chauffeur and all round right-hand man'. Baba has five cars and sensibly lives in what was once a maharaja's summer palace.

Eventually a motor trip to Baba is fixed up (with Dr. Gokok teed up in the back seat) and Baba ('just the suggestion of a pot belly') babbles away with Dr. Gokok freely translating.

But it seems that Baba is only human after all, for when Raj Reddy nips off to his grandmother's funeral, he returns to find a very sulky Baba ('Who did you choose, me or a corpse?'). Never mind, the photographs of chubby Baba are all sunny smiles, whether relaxing in his private quarters, receiving flowers presented by an enormous elephant, or standing proudly beside vast, genial, reliable and gig-lamped Dr. Gokok.

Critic's Corner: Gentlemen
WINNING WAYS

The Infirm Glory. By Godfrey Winn (Joseph, 1967).

It seems, so personal is the style and so vast has been the output, as though Godfrey Winn has already written as many autobiographical books as Compton Mackenzie but in fact this is the first. It is the Book Society's Alternative Choice. It has arrived with the maximum of advance publicity. It takes the author only to the beginning of the last war and we are promised another volume for whatever years may remain. It contains well over 100,000 words, but perhaps it is unfair to blame a journalist for the fatal flow with which the sentences gush (unfortunate verb) forth.

As literature it is a curate's egg of a book. The edible parts are sometimes remarkable, as when he forces himself to view his adored mother dead and in her coffin:

> I had been assured so often that in death, when all pain is over at last, the wracked features resume a beauty, often a more ethereal beauty than they have possessed in life. To comfort and reassure the mourner, always.
>
> But I was to discover, horribly, that this is a false myth. Was this witch-like creature, whose lips seemed to be twisted into a final protesting grimace, my mother? I dropped the flowers and fled.

He writes honestly, and even with some sympathy and understanding, of his appalling black sheep father. It was the usual drab tale of extravagance, failure, the bottle, money-lenders, and unknown ladies entertained at the Trocadero and it took the family from a modish Birmingham suburb to a back street in East Sheen. It also took away Godfrey Winn's chance of going to Rugby and, possibly, Cambridge. It explains entirely the determination to become rich and independent, to be famous, and to do good, roughly I would think in that order of priority.

And it has all worked out. He is a phenomenon, the highest-paid English journalist of his kind in history and on nodding terms with both Royalty and the dustman. It all began at the moment when he found that articles on such subjects as 'The

Girls will be Girls

daughter I would like to have', 'Why the young are bad-tempered', and 'Have we failed the Dead?' were acceptable to the cheap (I speak financially) magazines. He has been at it in one way or another ever since, first striking it really rich with his Cudlipp-invented sugar-coated Personality Parade in the *Daily Mirror* in the thirties.

A mystery remains. To whom are his comfortable words addressed? Bachelor girls? Spinster men? The Hastyburger munchers in their bed-sitters? The lonely? The old and credulous? Widowed mothers, confident that he can remove both their tears and their rheumatism? Mr. Winn has an explanation for his popularity.

> I did possess something that was to manifest itself equally in my early published writings. A kind of directness of appeal which owed nothing to art or professional skill, everything to my instinctive eagerness to communicate.

Lord Beaverbrook, for whom he worked for a dozen years, had an answer too (in a phrase which even his subject could not have bettered): 'He shakes hands with people's hearts.'

Mr. Winn is brave enough to quote blistering attacks in the pages of the *New Statesman* by an unmellow Cyril Connolly on his first two novels, *Dreams Fade* and *Squirrel's Cage* ('An anthologist would not know where to begin were he to select a paragraph for an Oxford Book of English Slop'). This is disarming but not completely so for Mr. Winn has stubbornly refused to learn that what can sit happily on the pages of a newspaper just will not do between the covers of a book. With him the gossip-writer is ever lurking, waiting to pounce, whether it is about Dorothy Ward ('Where is her equal in tights today?'), or Princess Margaret ('I can't imagine anything more wonderful than being who I am'), or the Duchess of Windsor ('Somehow we have made our own private happiness').

Despite wise advice from Somerset Maugham, of whom he gives a substantial sketch (perhaps the best thing in the book), Mr. Winn's taste in words is immature. He has not advanced. With his rumly youngish looks he has retained his boyish style. Schoolmasters will reach for their red ink. A simple word

Critic's Corner: Gentlemen

alarms him, and so 'to marry' is 'to exchange vows', to meet is to encounter, to live is to dwell, very tired is utterly spent, a joke is a sally, London is the metropolis, and Fate is inscrutable. He refers, twice, to 'The whirligig of time', and not with a smile. There is a deplorable sentence which begins 'The sleeping landscape crystallized under the aurora of the untarnished moon'.

Nobody capable of any self-mockery could write such things and it must, alas, be said that when the good fairies were handing out humour, Godfrey Winn had been called to the telephone. Humour would have lightened the many pages on which his less close relations appear in such dismaying profusion. A sense of humour would have made him see the ludicrous side of the footnotes with which he kindly explains some of the names: Juliet Duff (Lady Juliet Duff), Pamela Berry (Lady Pamela Berry), Catherine Willoughby (Lady Catherine Willoughby), Ursie Filmer Sankey (Lady Ursula Filmer Sankey). And a sense of fun might have softened some of the rather defiant overconfidence, a failing which kind people often try to attribute to shyness. But then not everybody is kind.

His title is a quotation from T. S. Eliot. Let us allow Mr. Winn to explain it, and have the last word. It is now 1939.

> Nearly fifteen years had passed. I had seen so much, listened and recorded many stories that were, indeed, far stranger than fiction. I had encountered the famous and the infamous, the noble ones and the unknown. On my part, I had achieved much by material standards, and yet, in other ways, so little. How brief, how infirm for me had been the glory.

The Positive Hour. By Godfrey Winn (Joseph, 1970).

To be asked to help choose the Post Office Girl of the Year would go to almost anybody's head, I do see, but it is remarkable that Godfrey Winn's publisher should consider his life of sufficient importance to enshrine it in three volumes. Volume III ('Here is My Space') is announced as being in active preparation, and though Volume II is less of a worry than Volume I,

Girls will be Girls

the disadvantages remain, together with the sadly unacceptable boastfulness (though not about his stouthearted war efforts), as if to make a fortune from glib journalism and to know the Hon. Gloria Smartyboots were, somehow, praiseworthy.

    I wonder if other authors have the feeling which often assails me, that everyone else seems to write so much more arrestingly than oneself.

Er, yes. The reason is clear. 'At my birth I was granted the gift of total recall.' For a writer, this is not a gift, it is a disaster. Out pour the trivialities, the remembered (I suppose) conversations. Out gush the words, and what words they are. People 'rejoinder', tired people are 'drained'. One encounters, one is attired in uniform, one maintains the exchange of banter. One speaks of 'yesterday's memories tinted by Time'. How can Mr. Winn go on calling London 'the metropolis'? Does his ear tell him *nothing*? And out, too, gush the names: Lady Mountbatten ('But don't you see, Godfrey . . ?'), A. V. Alexander ('Don't you see, Godfrey . . ?'), Lord Mountbatten ('Look, there's the Crown of India, Godfrey'), Lord Beaverbrook ('Capital, Godfrey, capital'). But if Mr. Winn is going in for names, he really must get them right. Lynn Fontanne's name is mis-spelt twice, and in the index she appears also as 'Mrs. Mildred Lunt'. Miss Fontanne is certainly Mrs. Lunt, but Mr. Lunt was christened Alfred and not Mildred.

CHRISTMAS REVIEWS OF BOOKS FOR GIRLS

1956

Strange Quest at Cliff House. By Nancy Moss (Chambers).
Valerie of Gaunt Crag. By Elizabeth Hyde (Chambers).
Theo and her Secret Societies. By Margaret Rowan (Chambers).
Two Girls in a Boat. By C. Salter (Blackie).
The New Girl at Melling. By Margaret Biggs (Blackie).

THOUGH this year's schoolgirl stories are milk-and-water when compared with the Brazilian glories of yesteryear, there are indications that authoresses are once more concentrating on the sensible, basic subjects such as lying, cheating, squabbling, and shinning up and down creepers.

In *Strange Quest at Cliff House*, Miss Nancy Moss gives us the third of her splendid Cliff House yarns. Devilish Irene Fletcher is still head girl and has now instituted fagging, sharply crushing all opposition: 'How dare you raise your voice to me! Another word and I will take you straight to Miss Pusey.' There are still no cricket-pitches or tennis-courts, and the Black Sheep (a chic society of the smarter prefects) are 'dedicated to keeping Cliff House School the slack and degenerate school' it has previously been. In pursuit of this unusual aim they watch TV in the boxroom, steam open letters, and lure poor little Violet Starr on to Hermit Island, a naval gunnery practice area, where the startled junior comes in for a brisk bombardment.

The live-wire Miss Bolney arranges co-educational rambles (' "It's official", chortled Ann'), with a Roman pavement one day and two prehistoric stone circles the next, and Christine is all excitement when a sailing club is begun ('There's something in me that answers the call of the sea'). Susan Savage and Cissie Carew go sailing with Miss Bolney and no sooner are

Girls will be Girls

they out of harbour than water covers the floor boards ('Why, what's this? We're awash!'), the sail is hauled down ('Girls, you must bale!'), the water rises ('Good gracious!') and they look about for assistance ('Wave to the trawler, Cissie'). At sunrise upon the cliff top, and in a scene of great power, Beatrice Lamont, her face working convulsively, confesses that it was she who was responsible ('It was I who pulled out the bung, Miss Bolney'), Miss Bolney countering with 'In what way have I so gravely offended you?'. Poor Beatrice ('Don't get hysterical, Beatty') receives a tremendous wigging from Miss Pusey at prayers, leaving her 'statuesque and stricken' and, understandably, no longer a prefect.

Valerie of Gaunt Crag is chiefly remarkable for the complications of its plot. To Cornish Gaunt Crag, former residence of the rascally Silas Trevase, whose hidden treasure is being unwittingly guarded by a sizeable octopus, comes Valerie Peterson, whose blind, ex-R.N. father, widower of world-famous violinist, Athalie, is living incognito on a local house-boat after a spell of employment with smuggler Cork Dowling, and is now secretly *fiancé* to Miss Lenstead, who shares a photographic interest with Dr. Langford, whose son, Murray, 'has a cheery word for everyone' and rescues Valerie when she steers her bicycle ('Golly, I *am* being a bother!') into a pond, if you follow me.

Also prominent is Christine Masters, whose Aunt Cynthia is proprietress of the Half Moon Restaurant ('Aunt Cynthia never serves, as you know').

> Last summer, Christine had deliberately damaged Wynne Carter's violin ten minutes before she was due to compete before Sir Miles and Lady Craig and other school governors for the much-coveted Trocambria Trophy . . . Accomplished violinist as Wynne Carter was, being robbed of her beloved instrument at the last moment was a blow from which she was unable to recover.

Valerie, wrongly accused of blabbing to Miss Vaughan, has to parade in a sandwichboard with SNEAK on it, while the Fourth Form recites 'Here comes Valerie, Sneak of the School, the girl who broke the Golden Rule', after which trying experience poor

Christmas Reviews of Books for Girls: 1956 and 1957

Valerie blubs in the Marie Curie dorm ('She *is* taking it badly') and has to be calmed with cocoa. Did Valerie compete for the Trocambria Trophy? But of course; 'Miss Waller gave her a chord' and off she went into Wieniawski's *Légende*, raising it from 'the corporeal to the spiritual level', after which Lord (apparently) Craig leapt over the Judges' Table, and Valerie, 'physically and emotionally spent', slumped forward in a dead faint, Miss Whiting ('Fish' to the girls) looking sharp with the smelling salts.

Theo and her Secret Societies finds us at Blair Court on the south coast with June Surtees, Sandra Matlock, Cherry Heskwith, and Miss Bellows, Miss Batt and Miss Darkaritt. There is a good deal of hockey under Mrs. Kyre ('Pax! Pax! I can do no more!'), study beanos ('That was scrumptious cocoa, Kath') some forbidden night outings ('I'll drift up to bed earlyish and put a bolster in'), and the Drama Comp. with Candy Hoskins in pale sea-green net with a very full ballet-length skirt ('H'm, sounds lovely') and little Alyth Boone as Puck. The new girl, Theo Fleet, finds it all rather tame but she starts a Dare Club and there are other exciting wheezes:

> 'We could be pixies in the house and get up early to do things when everyone was asleep,' suggested Janet hesitatingly.
> They all turned to her with their eyes alight.
> 'The very thing!' cried Theo.

Theo has some ups and downs in popularity but eventually wins through ('One of the day girls offered her an open packet of potato crisps').

Two Girls and a Boat takes us into an east coast yachting world where Babs visits Jill who has got 'a simply gorgeous little dinghy' and knows all about gudgeons, pintles, sail tiers and how to rig a new backstay. Similarly well informed are Lady Alicia Bloggs, in a tight-fitting yellow jumper and puce velveteen slacks, and a mysterious Pole called Anton Wladislauw who lost his way in Colchester. A flash of gold teeth, a black beard, and here is a member of the secret police, Feodor Zabrowski, up to no good:

Girls will be Girls

'Hah!' yapped the visitor. 'I wish to buy a yacht. There is yachts to sell here, no?'

'No,' said Jill.

'Pssht!' said the man disgustedly –

and with a final 'Tcha!' he goes off to try his luck in Mersey. Lady Alicia takes the girls sailing and is ready with 'We'll goosewing the jib' in between shrieks of 'Lee-oh!' and 'Port gun'l'. Meanwhile, Zabrowski is seen behaving oddly in Clacton, Babs gets photographic instruction from Bill ('You are inclined to over-expose') and Anton's brother, Stefan, dives into the sea from a passing liner. 'Urr-humph' says Jill's father towards the end. Quite so.

In *The New Girl at Melling* (colours: green and gold), the headmistress, Miss Pickering, is described as being nervous and tender-hearted and is inclined to doodle on her blotting-pad, which really will not do *at all*. However, there is the music mistress, Miss Killegan, who plays 'New every morning is the love' at prayers, with her golden gypsy earrings swinging to the rhythm, and winds up with a sonata 'which she did not know very well'. When not at the keyboard, she tends to appear in a duffle coat and tartan trousers. Musical Anne Laurence falls foul of the maths mistress, cardigan-swathed Miss Saunders, and is sent to the library to write out fifty times 'I must try to control my disgusting rudeness'. Then, her mind awhirl with impots and music ('I played the Mozart this evening, you know'), she is discovered sleep-walking in her blue 'jamas. However, she is fully herself again after a few chromatic scales ('Just stop a mo and hear me play the Beethoven'), and in no time at all is playing the Purcell to Sir Stephen Pearce, fresh from the Proms and all attention: 'You've got something out of the ordinary, you know. Something in the touch—the feel. Can't analyse it, but it's there.'

CHRISTMAS REVIEWS OF BOOKS FOR GIRLS

1957

THE MIXTURE AS BEFORE

The Cliff House Monster. By Nancy Moss (Chambers).
If It Hadn't Been For Frances. By P. M. Warner (Collins).
The Young Horse Dealers. By Mona Sandler (Country Life).
Jump To The Stars. By Gillian Baxter (Evans).
Excitements at the Chalet School. By Elinor Brent-Dyer (Chambers).

> 'It's . . . it's uranium!' breathed Hilary, squatting behind the Pankhurst Pavilion and jabbing at the ominous grey substance with her lacrosse stick. So it had been true then, that little tell-tale twitch of her geiger counter during algebra, and Muriel watched enthralled as her chum deftly stuffed great handfuls of the valuable matter into her satchel. Then she tensed as Hilary's face, drained of all colour, swung towards her. 'There's only one way to make sure, though. Bung it into Miss Bellingham's reactor in Stinks Lab. We may . . .' here she caught her breath for a space, 'we may vaporise ourselves, but . . .' Swiftly banishing the thought of forming yet another dreaded mushroom, the two youngsters darted off, pigtails flying, towards the stately yellow pile that was the Edythe Castleton Laboratory.

Stories for girls should by now be chock-a-block with passages such as the above, with radio-active headmistresses on every side and strontium in the porridge, but authoresses haven't yet responded to this exciting challenge and we might as well not have struggled into the atomic age at all.

But who can complain when there is another Nancy Moss to cheer us? Characters in *The Cliff House Monster* divide up roughly into those who have glimpsed the Monster (cave-dwelling and with eyes like giant red wine-gums) and those who have missed this treat. Clara Figgins has seen it ('Quite an

Girls will be Girls

experience'). Vesta Carnilly hasn't seen it but her father has, from the air. Pale-faced Lilian Purdey ('I feel all wobbly') sees it and faints dead away. Then, while Alerdyce Bell is trying to take a happy snap of the Monster by night, Cissie and Susan pedal along the shore to prevent a kipnapping and Susan is nearly decapitated by an aeroplane ('I'd rather not talk about it if you don't mind'). For tampering with prefects' togs, Susan is seized, put into a sack, and in a voice 'vibrant with menace', Irene Fletcher (the wickedest head girl in the business) announces a flogging. The startled Susan kicks gamely out and registers a stinger on Martha Cray's shin, but is overwhelmed.

> 'Leave her to me!' snapped a menacing voice, and Felix, almost in one bound, leapt upon Susan, who, restricted by the sack, collapsed under her weight. 'Now,' snarled Felix, 'get your canes ready.'

In the end, Maud Draper replaces the demoted Irene ('She soon made her influence felt. She suggested table-tennis as an indoor game'), and the Monster turns out to be a fuel-less car, the invention of Raymond Poyntz, run by springs and requiring a complete rewinding every thirty miles.

In *If It Hadn't Been For Frances*, Frances and Deborah take a sea trip ('I feel a bit weird') to Holland ('We're going to enjoy ourselves or bust'). Dutch surprises abound: there is Haarlem ('Coo! There's a nun on a bicycle!'), Alkmaar ('Horses with chequered behinds'), Noordwijk ('I do love canals'), and Amsterdam ('The *hugest* pansies'). And there is the excitement of getting home to the cat ('Put it down, Frances, do. It wants to settle') and Miss Baring (centre parting, with a twist of brown plaits at the nape: cinnamon wool dress: brown sandals). Stand-offish Diana Templeton ('What a pill!') comes to stay, hurls all her shoes at pussy ('Filthy things!'), slops about in slacks wondering where the servants are, wears her flowered organdie at the Fete, but helps to water the wallflowers ('You're a sport, Di'). Little Deborah gets quite thoughtful about the Morgans, 'a most troublesome family—but extremely interesting psychologically'.

Christmas Reviews of Books for Girls: 1956 and 1957

How would it be, Deb's thoughts inquired of her, to be one of a family of nine, sleeping, somehow or other, on the top deck of an old bus? Mightn't it make you think differently, act differently, grow up, in fact, into a different kind of person?

See what you mean, Deb.

The Young Horse Dealers are Jean and Moyra, who invest Moyra's £200 ('Mummy, *please* don't stop us') in various quadrupeds and off we canter into the world of Dawn Wind (which is a horse), the Handy Pony Class, and that nice Mrs. Sykes calling people 'poppets'. Eventually even Daddy is won over and is saying 'I shouldn't mind a day out with the Boxford'. In that particular four-legged world, the following things appear to be desirable: sloping shoulders, heaps of bone, well let down hocks, dark dapples, and massive quarters. I can't quite make out whether 'plenty of feather on her legs' is nice or nasty. It doesn't *sound* very nice.

Jump To The Stars contains a devil-horse called Ember, with a Death notched up, who has thinly chiselled nostrils, through which he has the unlovely habit of snuffling out white froth over Helen's faultlessly cut jodhpurs. Never mind: there is a stallion at stud promisingly named Silver Fountain, and Mr. Cooper-Smythe on Southdown Dragonfly, and saddle sores and girth galls and stable stains. Finally, the heroine is offered a job as a groom-instructress and, naturally enough, resigns instantly from the Bognor Regis Secretarial College.

Excitements at the Chalet School vary. There is an avalanche ('A whacker to judge by the sound of it'), a past headmistress (Miss Bubb), a landslide, Miss Annersley in her crimson twin set, and Margot Maynard (forgetmenot eyes), who 'fell into Lucerne last March'. You'll want to know the school officers for the term: Head of Games—Blossom Willoughby; Responsible for Stationery—Lala Winterton; Second Hobbies Prefect—Lesley Bethune. Conversation is partly in French (*'Voulez-vous des order-marks?'*). Matron ('Matey') leads locker-raids on the Pansy Dormitory and then has an emotional upset and takes to her bed ('Shove in a couple of bottles'). Charmian Spense switches off all the lights during plain sewing with Mademoiselle ('Be quiet, *mes filles*! A fuse has blown'), has to apologise

Girls will be Girls

to the entire school after Prayers, and souses her pillow in an agony of remorse. Poor Yseult Pertwee is besotted with elocution and wants to specialize, but Mrs. Pertwee, lecturing in America on the Arthurian Legends, is against it:

> Mother knows how much her big girly wants to give more time to verse-speaking and acting, but really, pet, your work is so poor in other subjects that I feel I must stiffen my upper lip and be *firm*. So the answer is no.

My answer isn't exactly no. But it's in the y-y-y-yes category.

JUST AN ORDINARY TERM

1949

December 15th

Dearest Maud,

Term is nearly over and I look forward to our holiday beano at the Mecca and a thorough chin-wag. What years ago dear old Newnham seems!

As I write, the young things are out carol-singing. It is on the chippy side but they have their woollies and there will be cocoa. The evening is still and quiet and the sound of their clear voices uplifted in the High Street is strangely moving.

The American girl has made a great hit. I feared that her name (Martha Milton Zimmermann) might be against her, but when she announced that she came from Chicago they were all over her. She has been most generous: nylons for the Sixth (and yours truly!), refrigerated steaks all round, and fearsome concoctions called Rye and Bourbon which have caused much merriment in the studies. She showed them how to wire a chair for electricity, and they put a sharp charge through Mademoiselle just as she was getting into her stride with a La Fontaine fable. The current was from the School plant, and obviously of no very damaging voltage, but Mademoiselle made the most ridiculous fuss and hopped about screaming 'au secours' until I begged her to stop. Sometimes one really despairs of foreigners. However, Cook ran up a delicious supper (omelette) and I soothed her with Jean Sablon on the portable: a nip of Dubonnet and soda at bed-time and she was herself by morning.

Our new mistress, on the other hand, has been an utter fiasco. Her name was Miss Luker (they called her 'Filthy' at once: how terribly quick girls are!) and she simply never found her feet. She could not distinguish between pranks and real naughtiness and kicked up Old Harry about a measly half-bottle of gin missing from her wardrobe. She completely lost her wool with Aileen Dunlop (holder of the Trumper Hygiene Cup for Upper Corridor) so they set fire to her clothes during

Girls will be Girls

Detention and sawed her bureau in two. I turned a blind eye and quietly wrote off to Chitty and Gale for a replacement—somebody cheery who likes a joke, with Zoology, Geology, Calculus, Russian and Handicrafts. November the Fifth was a merry affair, with bangs and explosions most of the day and a monster bonfire (of desks! but I didn't get ratty) as soon as dusk fell. One of the fireworks could not have been properly assembled and blew all the Vicarage windows out: it was just like dear old 1940! Our head girl (Rhoda Hornby, and a real fizzer), had a whip-round among the Juniors and soon netted the cash. She laughingly called it Entertainment Tax and everybody under fifteen had to stump up eighteen and sixpence. There was some grumbling but she scotched that pretty pronto! It was a fine example of leadership and initiative! Rhoda should make her mark at Girton.

The School Play went off splendidly. They did selected scenes from Shakespeare—murder of Duncan (Doreen simply A.I. as Lady M), murder of Banquo, murder of Caesar, Gloucester's eyes being put out, and Othello smothering Desdemona. Grizel Carver, who played Desdemona, fought back with such gusto that the thud of blows rather spoilt the balance of the piece but the audience cheered it to the echo and demanded an 'encore'! Matron was busy most of the evening with cuts and bruises, and Othello herself is in the San. with concussion and two black eyes (real ones this time!!!).

There have been, for once in a way, no serious mishaps this term, praise be. Little Joy Mowbray (*such* blue eyes) accidentally set fire to the Chapel last week, but apologised so prettily that I hadn't the heart to scold. I do feel that the battle is won when they are genuinely sorry, don't you? I have confiscated her lighter, however, and also the packet of Alura cigarettes that Matron spotted in her handkerchief drawer. I hate to make too many rules (look at Tudway Towers and all their tragic upheavals last spring!) but I did just say a word to the Juniors about not smoking in their cubicles. The danger of fire is a very real one.

      Cheerio till Friday,
        Yours,
         Madge.

THE PLEASURES OF READING

MARRIED BUT STILL PALS

The Top of the World. By Ethel M. Dell (Ernest Benn, reprinted 1961).
The Black Knight. By Ethel M. Dell (Ernest Benn).

Two new and handsome Ethel M. Dell reprints show the falsity of the idea that this prolific authoress, dead, alas, these twenty years, wrote chiefly for the attic-lodged, £12-a-year skivvy. Her public was an altogether wider but wholly feminine one, for Miss Dell's heroines prefer to live in a sort of married celibacy which a man might find irksome. They tease with a kiss, they ask to be chums only, they hover in a state of delicious indecision, and though their husbands seem equal to the demands made on their self-control, their eyes flash masterfully to indicate that they have something more elaborate in mind.

The heroines are firmly in the *de luxe* bracket. Ermine Devereux in *The Black Knight* is mistress of Rossingdon Manor but lives with her brother-in-law, Hildebrand Courtenaye of Courtenaye, and leads the county rather a dance (the wild Devereux blood, you know). For Sylvia Ingleton in *The Top of the World* Miss Dell has composed a memorable opening sentence: 'She stood in the great vinery—a vivid picture against a background of clustering purple fruit.' But Sylvia has annoyances. Her fiancé, Guy Ranger, is in South Africa, her stepmother is tyrannical ('Call me madam!') and, having the straightest seat for miles around ('Winnie carried me beautifully'), she is pursued by a loutish M.F.H. ('Cherry-ripe, you're lookin' spiffin' to-night. . . . You like diamonds, hey?').

Both girls find themselves, a trifle absent-mindedly, at the altar. Sylvia reaches the *veldt* and marries Burke, Guy's cousin, partly because he looks like Guy (now gone to the bad, aided by

Girls will be Girls

booze, morphia and extensive mammy-palaver) and partly because he met her at the station (I agree: nothing is nicer). Ermine hooks up almost overnight with Sam Gregory ('His face had the anaemic look of a plant raised in the dark') mainly because she, quite understandably, wants to put more space between herself and Hildebrand Courtenaye of Courtenaye (he is given to breathing heavily and calling her 'you infernal jade!'). Then, to the mounting irritation of the bridegrooms, Sylvia bends her thoughts to Guy, *delirium tremens* and all, and Ermine daydreams about a Black Knight who, at Carnival time on the Riviera, discouraged her from ending it all by impeding a *rapide* at the *gare*.

For Ermine, I'm sorry to say, has a past. Outstandingly unsuccessful at the roulette tables, she fell into the clutches of rascally, orgy-arranging Emilie Silver, the curse of Mentone, and was parcelled out to a beast in human shape who had never heard of orange blossom and who briskly put paid to Ermine's innocence and her debts, in that order ('When I got restive, he gave me cocaine'). The beast, incidentally, is now a Major and has the V.C.—the *unfairness* of everything!

Marital relations are a mockery, both girls fainting dead away at the drop of anything at all. 'I like a man to be just a jolly comrade,' says Sylvia, maddening Burke by blowing cigarette smoke all over him 'through laughing lips'. Burke, his eyes full of 'burning hunger-light', obligingly calls her 'little pal' or 'partner'. Ermine may indeed be 'a traveller in life's journey who has pressed on too hard' but, with less to lose, so to speak, she is equally unscrupulous. One peck from Sam and she becomes a marble image, despite whole hog encouragements from a Gypsy Deborah ('Offer it up, dearie. Give willing. Old Deborah knows').

A hint of togetherness and Ermine either 'feigns slumber' or pointedly requests solitude ('Why don't you go out and shoot something?'). They dilly and they dally, Sylvia until the penultimate chapter when, with Guy safely dead, 'she gave of her all in full and sweet surrender.' Ermine cuts it even finer, giving of *her* all on the penultimate page, and only then because it turns out that weedy Sam was the Black Knight all the time.

The Pleasures of Reading

Of the two original situations, perhaps virginal Sylvia's is the more agitating and copiously she reacts to it. Her heart beats 'like the labouring of clogged machinery', she palpitates, she reels, she repeatedly sees things through mists, her eyelids flutter, her throat works and her pulses race. Her bosom? It heaves and has an important door-key thrust into it for safety. Still, it's nice to know she has no servant problem.

> She looked up and saw an old Kaffir woman carrying a basin. 'This is Mary Anne,' said Burke. 'A useful old dog except when there is any dope about! Hope you don't mind niggers.'
> 'I shall get used to them,' said Sylvia rather faintly.

She does indeed, lashing out at one of them with a *sjambok*, but skilfully retaining her ability to swoon when Burke suggests something really distasteful to a sensitive girl.

A KIND OF JELLY

A Clip of Steel. By Thomas Blackburn (MacGibbon & Kee, 1969).

The clip of steel of Mr. Blackburn's title was a Swiss anti-wet-dream device (as supplied to monastic orders and pugilists), a contraption with metal spikes which, when snugly in position, sharply discouraged Nature's startling preliminaries. It was sent to him at school by his father, a slightly dusky-skinned country vicar who, born and brought up in Mauritius, had a neurotic fear that somewhere along the line there had been a touch of the tar brush (his son, aged six, endured nightly bleachings with lemon juice and peroxide). He had two obsessions, colour and sex (absence of) and, though full of worldly innocence (the terrier puppy was named 'Pox'), did not hesitate to pass on some questionable information about adolescent perils:

Girls will be Girls

Your brain is full of grey matter, a kind of jelly. Touch yourself in that evil way and this jelly will leak down your spine and go to waste. I've seen boys in France and Mauritius who did this wicked thing, did worse things, sucked each other's 'tea-pots', torn from home and carried off to the lunatic asylum screaming.

The dread of sex was partly hereditary (his own father kept a bath of cold water handy and plunged in whenever Eros stirred) but the Rev. Blackburn was not even cosy in everyday matters. He sulked at tennis. He administered savage chastisements. If crossed in any way he sank dramatically into a chair with a cry of 'my blood pressure!' He even took umbrage when during an illness a nurse prudently wore a mask while ministering to him on the commode.

Exposure to this frightful parent brought results in his son that could be foreseen, a series of misdemeanours and rebellions, winding up at Cambridge. Here Thomas Blackburn decided not to confine his activities to any narrow academic syllabus. Entertaining, with friends, three *filles de joie* in his rooms in college, he later pressed a fiver into their hands and led them (the time was 2 a.m.) to the door of the Master's Lodgings, telling them that they had but to ring the bell to find an all-night taxi-service in full operation. The resulting cross-purposes conversation does not, alas, survive. Then an errant *capote anglaise* found its way into the hands of some self-righteous ordinands who sneaked, and Mr. Blackburn was sent down, punctuating the Master's strictures by taking pot-shots at him with his cherished china *objets d'art* ('I got him with the third as he was whisking through the door').

Mr. Blackburn has certainly had his share of life's demanding warp and woof. Even when happily housed with a lively French girl he discovered that on her less sedate days she would gaily rip open the flies of bus conductors and bring comfort to lonely Polish seamen among the trees in Green Park.

The Pleasures of Reading
D*MN *ND BL*ST

Dr. Bowdler's Legacy. By Noel Perrin (Macmillan, 1970).

It has ever been both a hopeless and an impertinent task to try to impose alleged standards of decency on others. Fashions change and time passes. Today's cry of 'Bugger!' is tomorrow's 'Drat!' Prudery is so much a matter of age, environment and class. In Lambeth pubs the loudest and most thunderous farts go quite unnoticed, whereas the smallest hiccough causes red faces all round and volleys of 'Pardon'. Prostitutes, asked by their clients to kiss them, are said to be horrified by such a disgusting suggestion and pass rapidly on to much more elaborate items on their menus. Yet in Edgbaston and S.W.1 the mouth would certainly be considered a more reputable organ than the anus. It's all according, and in our permissive society progress is not so much marching on as marching backwards. To observe upon a city pavement a closely entwined couple trying to swallow each other is merely to be wafted back two centuries. The next decade may even see the dreaded students indulging in open copulation at 'Request' bus stops, and who by then will greatly care?

You hear a whirring noise? Undoubtedly it is the Bowdlers (and so *many* of them) revolving in their graves. Though they could comfortably have formed a lacrosse team, there was no time for such giddiness with all that disapproving, erasing, substituting, cutting and cobbling to get through. The family operated from Bath and proudly spanned three generations, publishing their cleansed classics for over eighty years. In addition to Dr. Bowdler (he gave up medicine at 31 with a physical aversion to sick people), there were his parents (Squire Bowdler, a great reader-aloud, could effortlessly expurgate at sight), his sisters, Jane and Harriet (the latter found ballet dancing so indelicate that she kept her eyes shut throughout), his brother John, and his three nephews, all of them possessing the correct mixture of prudery and zeal which leads to really hearty expurgations. In addition, they were all blessed with extremely dirty minds.

Like a pack of hounds, they fell upon the national bard and

Girls will be Girls

tore him to pieces. In 1807 their *Family Shakespeare* appeared (they always published anonymously), with large sections of *Hamlet* missing and that depraved and licentious play, *Romeo and Juliet*, gone altogether. The shockable Harriet even went further and gaily lopped off any passages that she happened to find boring. Though Shakespeare had been tampered with before, the Bowdlers opened the flood gates and for the next hundred years mucking Shakespeare about became a happy pastime. Charlotte M. Yonge did an edition for schools. The secretary of the Working Men's College did one for working men. Lewis Carroll started on one for (surprise, surprise) young girls.

The Victorians, who made the state of being shocked a social asset, ensured that the expurgation industry roared ahead. The Bible had to go through it too. A splendid lady, the well-named Mrs. Trimmer, managed to wind her way primly through those rum events connected with the genial host of Sodom, Lot. Then John Bellamy learnt Hebrew and, frenziedly re-translating, discovered that Ham did not find Noah drunk and naked in his tent. Noah was fully clothed and had had just the one glass of wine (the first vintage since the Flood—possibly a rough and unassuming claret). And it goes without saying that poor old Onan's splashy activities got thoroughly tidied up.

Through all of this Noel Perrin is a marvellous guide—scholarly, lively and extremely funny. And on the idiocies went. William Alexander, not liking the passage in Leviticus about priests with crushed testicles, gave them ruptures instead. Noah (Dictionary) Webster decreed that Egyptians should have hind-parts rather than buttocks. Rossetti cut 'womb' out of Whitman and there was a fine old muddle over the word 'twat'. It was used, quite innocently, by Browning, and when the editors of the OED asked him what it might be, they received the answer that it means 'a piece of headgear for nuns'. It doesn't.

The Pleasures of Reading
CHEERIOSKI!

Posts-Mortem: The Correspondence of Murder. By Jonathan Goodman (David & Charles, 1971).
The Victorian Woman. By Duncan Crow (Allen & Unwin, 1971).

In the field of murder, women are more effective as victims than as executants. They are more trusting, more fragile, more choppable and more disposable. Not that disposal presents, these days, any problem (parcel your portions neatly and consign them to any form of public transport, confident that the portions will either be lost or stolen or so long delayed as to become unrecognizable).

Women are also more gullible. Take the case of Irene Munro, but recently deflowered by a saucy Frenchman ('I have booked balcony stalls for *Chu Chin Chow*, you naughty little girl'), and now holidaying alone, snug in white calico combinations, on the South Coast ('I'm not in love with Eastbourne yet'). Two chunky ne'er-do-wells invite her for a stroll along the Crumbles and off they saunter, Irene wisely bolstering her modest charms with a bag of goodies, of which the doomed trio freely partake. She also foolishly carried an expensive-looking bag, and, when found, her corpse was fully clothed, insultingly enough.

And what of Phyllis Dimmock, given to entertaining male paying guests while her husband was shunting about serving Brown Windsor in a Midland Railway restaurant-car, and who was found in Camden Town slit ear to ear and surrounded by empty bottles of stout? She had invited her murderer in to a tasteful supper for two ('Come dear, another gherkin?'). Public interest in this meaty affair was such that when a popular suspect was found innocent, Mrs. Beerbohm Tree rushed excitedly out on to the stage during a performance of *Julius Caesar* and gasped out the verdict to loud cheers. Tree's thoughts on this *coup de théâtre* have not been recorded.

And then there was poor Charlotte Cheeseman who, with her love for a soldier and her job in an East End cigar factory, ranks as the Carmen of Hoxton. To entice back her reluctant lover, she erupted into verse:

Girls will be Girls

> My pen is blunt, my ink is pale,
> My love for you will never fail.
> Apples is ripe, pears is better,
> George, dear, will you answer this letter?

George's crisp answer was to take her for a short walk on Tottenham Marshes where the evening's work earned him a sort of fame as the last murderer to be executed in Newgate.

By concentrating on the correspondence of these and other assorted persons, Mr. Goodman brings out the pitiful, often sordid, futile and humdrum nature of their lives. The nymphomaniac Starr Faithfull (a real name, though it sounds like a Hugh Walpole invention) liked to end her letters with the jolly word 'Cheerioski'. The Anglo-Indian Augusta Fullam, busy poisoning her husband, sent regular progress reports to her lover ('I give half a powder every day in his Sanatogen'). The fiancé-murderer of Maria Marten, once out of that red barn, firmly grasped the rule that Somebody Somewhere Wants a Letter From You ('We are both well, hoping it will find you the same'). There are also many of the Thompson-Bywaters letters, as painfully moving to read across the years as they were in 1922. Thank God *that* kind of mercilessness can never happen again.

Many of Duncan Crow's Victorian women would doubtless have welcomed murder. The average girl, roughly brought up in the incestuous mugginess of an over-crowded bedroom ('the first step to the Haymarket', boomed the *Saturday Review*) had little chance: ceaseless childbearing awaited her, or sweated labour in a factory, or horror in the mines. No wonder that so many of them chose, indeed, the Haymarket, up and down which they squeaked in their Balmoral boots, while along Piccadilly there was Sodom in Half Moon Street and Gomorrah in the Burlington Arcade (clients could be entertained on the upper floors of bonnet shops).

Though Victorian guilt about sexual activities is with us still, it was paradoxically the heyday of special treats, thwackings particularly. Thirteen-year-old virgins were apparently in ceaseless supply at £5 a go. Sadism was rife. Daughters were regularly whipped, their fathers helpfully suggesting improved methods:

The Pleasures of Reading

Nothing like leather! Cut a strap into strips and let your governess tie your daughter down upon an ottoman after evening prayers; the strap thus cut may be depended upon to inflict acute suffering.

Victorian prudery closed its eyes to much, a prudery that was as nothing compared to the American version. Theresa Yelverton, a gifted reciter, found herself, when in the U.S., forced to declaim an amended version of a favourite piece, the *Wreck of the Hesperus*:

> She struck where the white and fleecy waves
>   Looked soft as carded wool;
> But the cruel rocks they gored her side,
>   Like the horns of a gentleman cow.

PUTNEY PUZZLE

At The Pines. By Mollie Panter-Downes (Hamish Hamilton, 1971).

Has there ever, either in fact or in fiction, been a puzzle as baffling as The Mysterious Affair at The Pines? By what wizardry or mesmeric power did walrus-moustached literator and solicitor's son, Theodore Watts-Dunton, spirit away pleasure-loving red-haired free-thinking poet Swinburne (odd offspring of an Admiral and an Earl's daughter) from the heady environs of Russell Square and incarcerate him for life in a semi-detached villa in the then slightly common suburb of Putney?

The actual abduction in 1879 is perhaps comprehensible. Swinburne, aged 42, financially unsound and in the throes of *delirium tremens*, was in no position to put up a fight:

> He had wrecked his health and nearly died through what the Dictionary of National Biography, primly pursing its lips and then opening them just wide enough to permit the useful word to sidle out, called 'imprudences'. These were brandy, rackety

companions, and, at one period, visits to an establishment in St John's Wood's then dubiously respectable groves, where, in luxurious rooms, a couple of blonde Amazons flagellated the cutomers who were prepared to pay handsomely for such special pleasures.

Swinburne, acutely sensitive even through the alcoholic fumes, may also have been aware that in social circles he had become something of a handful:

> His hosts, if they were in the know, hid or kept a sharp eye on the liquor. For those who did not, the evening was apt to be punctuated by loud falsetto chanting and Terpsichorean displays, terminating in a sudden thump. Meanwhile the duns gathered at the door and everything got in a frightful mess. Important letters, manuscripts, agreements, all rose up in the Bloomsbury air like Alice's pack of cards and vanished.

No, the abduction itself is no problem but, once restored to health and an orderly life, what on earth held this highly-strung genius in S.W.15 (modern minds, over-absorbed with sex, can straightway rule out that activity)?

Pleasures there were, it is true, at The Pines. There was the solid comfort (for Watts-Dunton) of knowing that the house's lease forbade the building being used either as a house of ill-fame or as a lunatic asylum (though the dog, an inane woolly hearth-rug called Dido, gazes at the photographer in a manner that is plainly unhinged). There was Watts-Dunton's healthful curriculum for his famous and adored guest: this included walks on Putney Heath and chats with the pram-borne babies (so unhelpful that the only rhyme for 'babe' was 'astrolabe'), followed by roast mutton and apple-pie, washed down by a mini-bottle of Bass's pale ale.

There was, too, Watts-Dunton's nephew, perky little Bertie Mason ('the sweetest thing going at any price') to drool over in the modish Victorian manner and to write poems to (over 50 of them, all as printable as they are unreadable). Occasionally there were well-supervised visits from admirers (Max Beerbohm's account is well known) come to take luncheon with a legend. There were readings from Dickens, and an early bed. No brandy, no dancing, no flesh-tingling thwackings. And even when Watts-Dunton, aged 73, suddenly married Clara Reich (29), on Swinburne hung. Why?

The passages quoted above will have revealed Miss Panter-Downes's quality. Nobody could have dealt more wittily or sympathetically with a subject that has so many hilarious sides to it. Her researches into this supremely rum Putney pair have been brilliantly successful.

FLIPPERTY-FLOP

Pin-Up's Progress. By Richard Wortley (Panther, 1972).
Pegasus Descending. By James Camp, X. J. Kennedy and Keith Waldrop (Collier-Macmillan, 1972).

In *Pin-Up's Progress*, Richard Wortley, a dedicated social historian, examines a hundred years of pin-ups and writes in a splendidly unstuffy manner:

> A last look at progress finds vulvas still having a thin time but gentle tufts of pubic hair had curled their way into *Playboy* by January 1971.

Helpfully illustrated, we find something for everybody (for those interested in gentlemen's genitals, a muscled model strikes a *pose galante* on page 96). There is a sufficiency of vast bosoms and large, bare, female buttocks, so especially dear to the male heart, or something. Why were naked bottoms found particularly aphrodisiac when closely associated with bicycles? The leather saddles, perhaps? That pump at the ready position? Miss Clothilde, seen backview about to mount her Rudge-Whitworth on what must have been rather a sultry day, is rightly named 'A Fair Scorcher'. Titles have in general deteriorated. Saucy postcards, sixty years ago, were far more teasingly labelled—'It's Coming Down', 'Oh! That Garter!', and 'Interrupted Catching Crabs'.

We learn much. White knickers are best for photographic purposes, as black ones tend to look like blurred-out pubic

Girls will be Girls

hair. Early pin-ups were by no means confined to Gaiety Girls and even included W. G. Grace, whose likeness was tastefully woven in pink silk. Prudes found nudity acceptable provided the lady was disclosed either stepping out of a Classical garment or leaning against a column. How boring the last war's ebulliently busty girls, each indistinguishable from the other, seem in comparison with Mlle Polaire, who stirred all imaginations in 1915 with her 17-inch waist, her turban, her demure expression, and the ornamental ring which she wore through her nose.

Pegasus Descending, 'a treasury of the best bad poems in English', acknowledges its debt to Wyndham Lewis's *The Stuffed Owl* but does not need to duplicate it, so rich is the field. The editors start with a selection of worst opening lines, among them Hardy's 'Recall it you?/Say you do!' and Edward Mills's 'Sleep, my little papoose;/Thy father hunteth the moose'. And how merry to find Emily Dickinson, in her poem about the dying tiger, referring dramatically to his eyes as 'His Mighty Balls'.

William McGonagall (such an *output*, apart from its excellence) figures freely, together with Ella Wheeler Wilcox. One's own choice alights on three relatively unknown songbirds. First, James McIntyre who wrote a rhapsody to a four-ton prize cheese, displayed in Toronto in 1855:

> We have seen thee, queen of cheese,
>   Lying quietly at your ease,
>   Gently fanned by evening breeze,
>   Thy fair form no flies dare seize.

Then there is Sydney Dobell's memorable

> Oh the wold, the wold,
>   Oh the wold, the wold;
> Oh the winter stark,
>   Oh the level dark,
> On the wold, the wold, the wold!

The poem contains 35 more 'wolds' and is appropriately entitled WIND. And lastly, and perhaps the best, Theodore Marzials' lyrical description of a suicide by drowning:

The Pleasures of Reading

>Death!
>Plop.
>The barges down in the river flop
>Flop, plop.

It ends:

>Drop
>Dead.
>Flip, flop,
>Plop.

DARK COURTYARDS

Jack the Ripper. By Robin Odell (Harrap, 1965).
Autumn of Terror. By Tom Cullen (Bodley Head, 1965).

It is fortunate for the morbid that Jack the Ripper remains so named despite these fresh attempts to pin down his identity. To discover that he was *né* Hubert Merryweather or Algernon Beamish would at once remove some of his bizarre fascination. How many victims was he able to notch, so to speak, up? Five seems the likely bag, the entire *oeuvre* being completed in ten weeks and within one square Whitechapel mile. The 'sisters of the abyss' thus despatched were sadly expendable, but murdered women were then no rarity and Mr. Cullen has discovered contemporary females who were kicked to death, jumped on till crushed, chopped, sprinkled with vitriol or just set on fire. What set these apart was the prostitution, the preliminary throat-cutting, the darkness and blood, the haste and yet the *thoroughness* (it took two surgeons seven hours to reassemble Mary Kelly). The highest in the land was intrigued and weighed in, from Balmoral, with helpful advice: 'All these courtyards must be lit, and our detectives improved.'

The population of East London was at that time greater than either Berlin or St. Petersburg. Detection was indeed a problem and the newspapers urged that Shoreditch pugilists and the

Girls will be Girls

less hairy policemen should rig themselves up as you-know-whats and loiter enticingly about, 'wearing round their necks steel collars made after the style of a ladies' collaret'. This equipment would afford some protection before the misplaced gynaecologist could move to the main business of the meeting.

There was no lack of suspects. General Booth thought it was his own secretary, and Sickert plumped for a consumptive veterinary student. A Cardiff medium singled out a mustachioed Bolton farmer, and a retired Worthing blacksmith went further ('The Ripper was my Cousin Frank'). *The Times* suggested 'a foreigner engaged in the *charcuterie* trade', the *Star* being more precise with the strikingly apposite name of Cutbush, a noted Broadmoor fetishist. Mr. Odell seems to favour a psychopathic Jewish ritual slaughterman, while Mr. Cullen settles for a suicided barrister called Druitt (at one time Prefect of Chapel at Winchester). Was it conceivably not a man at all but a Jill the Ripper, a crazed, lesbian midwife connected with an abortion racket? She might well have the confidence of her prey and would know, professionally, her way about. Both authors discuss fully the endless and macabre possibilities in what must surely now be the final books on this gruesome hanky-panky.

LET HER PASS

The Real Isadora. By Victor Seroff (Hutchinson, 1972).

Isadora Duncan is steadily becoming as unwisely overexposed as T. E. Lawrence. In both cases the lives were a mess and the modest achievements simply do not stand up to such repeated scrutiny. I suspect that their interest owes much to those early and dramatically motorized deaths (for the forgetful, in 1927 Miss Duncan's scarf caught in a Bugatti wheel, breaking her neck). If only both these blown-up persons were still alive and living in wheezy and arthritic retirement in Bournemouth, we should be spared much of this ceaseless tra-la-la.

The Pleasures of Reading

How good a dancer was Miss Duncan? There can be few alive who saw her at her best. But of what did this American's best consist? To some, those bare or sandalled feet tell a dreary Terpsichorean tale; one is reminded yet again of Joyce Grenfell's splendidly breathless 'Go With The Music' *danseuse*. She appears to have been entirely self-taught. Mr. Seroff, in his detailed and generally adulatory biography, never mentions rehearsal hours. When, after appearing as a Californian Faun in Chicago's Masonic Roof Garden, she pressed on, harried by debts, to New York, the critics showed how signally she failed to set the Hudson on fire:

> Miss Duncan's costume for yesterday's dance was a species of surgical bandage of gauze and satin of the hue of raspberry ice, with streamers of various lengths, which floated merrily or mournfully as the dancer illustrated the bridal of Helene or the burial of Adonis.
>
> Miss Duncan's melancholy brother kindly read extracts from Theocritus and Ovid as an accompaniment to the writhings and painful leaps and hops of his sister, while a concealed orchestra discoursed doleful music and the audience of tortured souls gazed at one another and blushed or giggled. When the final dance was finished, there was a sigh of relief that it was over and that Miss Duncan's bandages hadn't fallen off, as they threatened to do.

She was, in fact, rather a one for letting her bandages fall off. After her virginity had gone bang in Budapest, she slept around a good bit, acquiring children by Gordon Craig and Mr. Singer, of those sewing machines. The latter also provided yachts, houses, a holiday in balmy Paignton, and a girl's best friend (diamonds). And it was only then that Americans, in the shape of publishers, saw her autobiographically as a valuable asset (her burblings about Spiritual Vision were answered by 'Enough of your hifalutin ideas send love chapters make it spicy').

Nobody shunted more restlessly to and fro. In Russia she tried to seduce Stanislavsky and married an avant-garde poet. In Paris she hopped to Chopin at soirées (*'Quel ravissement!'*). At frontiers during the Kaiser's War, sentries, she tells us, cried 'It is Isadora; let her pass'. In Boston, she bared her breasts with a shriek of 'This, this is beauty!' Some called her 'Isadorable', but on the other hand, some did not. Enveloped in a red shawl, she pranced to the Marseillaise, and as to her interpretation of Cesar Franck's 'Redemption', one would require rather more for the price of one's *fauteuil*:

> While the orchestra performed the score, Isadora at first simply lay on the stage, as if stricken down by a terrible blow; then she slowly rose from that position to her full height, and with outstretched arms toward Heaven and God, hands filled with goodness and charity, she remained motionless to the end of the composition.

Well, you can fool some of the people . . .

WOOLFS' LAIR

A Boy at the Hogarth Press. By Richard Kennedy (Heinemann, 1972).

When in 1928 sixteen-year-old Richard Kennedy was requested, because of sluggish scholastic progress, to leave his public school, he was rescued by Leonard and Virginia Woolf who were then on the look-out for 'a likely lad' to assist them in their Hogarth Press publishing activities and in due course he was taken on as apprentice publisher (doubling the role with office boy and general factotum). It was not mentioned to him that the life-span of the Woolfs' likely lads was on the brief side.

Marlborough's loss was the Woolfs' gain, and indeed ours, for the sharp-eyed Mr. Kennedy (now a distinguished artist) missed none of his employers' unguarded and unbuttoned moments and now gives us a fine picture of this unusual couple *en pantoufles* and *en* a rather whiffy Bloomsbury basement.

The basement housed the treadle printing machine on which Mrs. Woolf's novels were set up and printed, the counter where booksellers came to collect batches of them, the stocks of apples so essential to Mr. Woolf's well-being, two secretaries (Mrs. Cartwright and Miss Belcher), a lavatory in a windowless cup-

The Pleasures of Reading

board with holes in the door ('this sort of thing does not matter if you are in the literary world'), and the Woolfs' spaniel, Pinker ('he seems to be suffering from worms and drags his bottom along the carpet').

The basement also housed Mrs. Woolf during her creative moments:

> Sitting in her little space by the gas fire, she reminds me of the Bruce Bairnsfather veterans of the War, surrounded by sandbags. She looks at us over the top of her steel-rimmed spectacles, her grey hair hanging over her forehead and a shag cigarette hanging from her lips. She wears a hatchet-blue overall and sits hunched up in a wicker armchair with her pad on her knees and a small typewriter beside her.

Basement life was pleasantly active. There was double-entry book-keeping to master. There was Pitman's course. There was errand-boys' sauce to combat. There were the exciting days when Mrs. Woolf had scored a hit ('It's all hands to the pumps with *Orlando*'). There was a wooden shelf to construct and erect (it subsequently descended with a jolly bang on Lord Oliver's nut). There were Leonard Woolf's shrieks of rage over the petty cash, and there was rest at eventide ('Had supper in the ABC and read Proust').

Who was afraid of Virginia Woolf? Well, quite a lot of people. 'I think she is rather cruel in spite of the kind, rather dreamy way she looks at you.' But in fact the Woolfs were very good to Mr. Kennedy. They took him to their country house, Rodmell (rather smelly), and they took him on picnics ('Vanessa Bell fell down a bank on her bottom and I guffawed'). They took him skating, they discussed Life, and there was that modish literary pastime, cricket:

> David Garnett gave us a very agreeable welcome and fed us on beer and sandwiches. We went to the pavilion where Clive Bell was holding forth about cricket being like a ballet . . . He approached the crease rather like Serge Lifar. He made a ridiculous sort of cow shot the first ball, was lucky to connect and scored a boundary, but when he was stumped he started to argue with the umpire in the most unsportsmanlike manner, making all sorts of allusions to Japanese literature.

Girls will be Girls

I expect you'll like to know who kept wicket—Desmond MacCarthy (and a bit of a duffer he was), with James Strachey at point.

Mr. Kennedy's book is excellent and all too short. Some of his lively illustrations are extremely funny. The Woolfs live again, but for those of us for whom the mere mention of the name Bloomsbury now sets off a *tic nerveux*, let that be that.

MIND YOUR MANNERS

Over the Teacups. Edited by Dulcie M. Ashdown (Cornmarket, 1973).
The Lady's Realm. Edited by Lady Georgina Coleridge (Hutchinson, 1973).
Not Without a Chaperone. By Cecil Porter (New English Library, 1973).

These delightful volumes, selections from the periodical magazines of the late Victorians and the Edwardians, still contain much of value for those of us who have to grapple gamely with life's challenges. Worried about a tasteful method of munching bread-and-butter while wearing gloves? Flora Klickman in *How To Behave* has the answer (only partake of it when *rolled*). Those spots before your eyes? Probably your veils are too elaborately decorated. Switch to a simpler and less demanding mesh. But how comforting for those of us with prominent chins to be assured, by a noted physiognomist, that our bowel movements are likely to be more reliable and vigorous than with those whose chins recede (sluggish performances, and valuable minutes wasted).

The upper crust, of course, did not need to be told how to hand a lady into a carriage, how to extract her, and how to cold-shoulder a lady who was not a lady (Mr. Porter recalls that doom-laden and dismissive phrase, 'I couldn't quite *place* her'). The magazine readers were, clearly, mainly women who, coming from 'The Larches' and 'The Laurels', found it thrilling in their middle-class world to learn what to do if Royalty 'signified

The Pleasures of Reading

their willingness to sojourn beneath your roof' for a week, especially if it were King 'Lock Up Your Married Daughters' Edward VII and Queen Alexandra (partial to japes and a dab-hand at apple-pie beds).

With the willingness duly signified, there's not the smallest need to panic—merely make ready fourteen bedrooms and six sitting-rooms for the royal suites and remember that eight courses (iced oyster soufflé is a must) for dinner is *quite* sufficient. Mrs. Waldemar Leverton will help you here with *Little Entertainments and How to Manage Them*. Oh and by the way, warn your other guests to bring *full* mourning in case of a sudden royal demise.

Healthful bicycling was beginning to be all the rage and Mrs. Thorneycroft of *Over the Teacups* is especially good on suitable kits for outings and is indeed to be seen herself, making good speed downhill on her 'Swift', in a rather showy cream chemisette with a heart-shaped mulberry bolero. Warmth while awheel was something of a problem. Should it be wash-leather knickers or tweed bloomers? In *Not Without a Chaperone*, Mrs. Danvers Delano, in a cleverly argued passage, opts decisively for bloomers.

The Lady's Realm specializes in thoughtful articles—'Is Bridge Immoral?', 'The poetry of Metal Work' and 'How to Defy the Cold' (benzoated lard for chaps, and cocoa butter to strengthen the eyebrows). Here too are some pleasing snaps—Phyllis and Zena Dare, the Silence Room at the Ladies' Automobile Club (empty, natch), a selection of outstandingly expendable Russian Grand Dukes, and a female hockey-match with the players tensed for the bully-off and the atmosphere electric.

Everywhere are hints for leading a happy and productive life. Before settling down at the English Organette (30s.) and pedalling out a few well-loved hymns, do freshen that strip of lino with a generous daubing of Hoskyn's Ben Trovato Paints (beige is such a pleasant shade), or give a 'lift' to your Cowes costumes by stitching on velvet fuchsias or humming-birds' feathers. And why not put paid to those unsightly pimples with a smearing of Dr. Mackenzie's arsenical soap? Then, exhausted, relax with one of the many daydream 'Storyettes' or with a

Girls will be Girls

section called 'How To Read The Face' (the lively drawing of 'An Idiot', all slobber and disaster, is a fine likeness of one of our older bishops). Or you can gaze at the photograph of a startled walrus, who turns out to be the King of Italy, or tremble at the spectacle of women prisoners at Wormwood Scrubs (they found, one is so happy and relieved to know, the Anglican Chapel such a *boon*).

Married happiness implies children and for them the seaside was particularly perilous:

> Paddling is a most injudicious and mischievous custom, as it makes the feet cold and sends the blood to the head. Children whose lips turn blue after bathing should be given ginger wine (keep a flask in the bathing-machine). Should a child's eyelids become inflamed, dab them with cornflower petals soaked in *white* brandy.

And try not to make difficulties where no difficulties are.

A hostess is for ever on the rack and one of her perpetual conundra is What To Do With Bores. Again we look with confidence to Mrs. Danvers Delano, that veritable volcano of clear thinking:

> A great many people, particularly in the country, are too uninteresting to entertain except at a garden party, and they look forward from year to year to their annual outing.

So 'dust the summer-houses', prepare eleven varieties of sandwich, engage a Hungarian orchestra, sponge the dovecots, make with the claret-cup, and rejoice in the knowledge that 'this form of entertainment looks much more than it really costs'. A short Grace from the vicar and away you go.

With George V, the Edwardian social scene, with its hair-raising class distinctions, disintegrated pretty sharply, as Mr. Porter points out:

> Towards 1914 the worm was already in the bud. More young women were entering offices, inflaming men with glimpses of their ankles. Headstrong girls were mocking their chaperones (was nothing sacred?). Freer 'American' manners were creeping

in, not so much this time with the enterprising Society brides dowered with steel, pork, oil and railroads but through Tango Teas and that disgraceful, cacophonous but highly popular show *Hullo Ragtime* at the London Hippodrome in 1912.

Shortly after, the shot that killed 20 million rang out at Sarajevo: and that, and really not a moment too soon, was that.

Lillie Langtry. By Noel B. Gerson (Hale, 1972).

When the British Public gives its interest and affection, it gives it like a dog, for life. The recipients of this evergreen adoration are varied indeed—lone yachtsmen, fish fingers, Anna Neagle, scampi in the basket, English lady tennis players thudding their way to yet another plucky defeat, Lillie Langtry, baked beans and Maharajahs.

And Edward VII too. The lustful royal carnivore, inventor of the least cordial and most expensive *entente* in our history, figures freely in Mr. Gerson's lively account of the Jersey Lily (such a *beefy* looking girl). She was certainly not just a pretty face, as Bernard Shaw discovered:

> I resent Mrs. Langtry. She has no right to be intelligent, daring and independent as well as lovely. It is a frightening combination.

It didn't frighten ordinary gentlemen and they went down like nine-pins. In America, crazed millionaires denuded Tiffany's *vitrines* on her behalf. In Europe, Crown Prince Rudolph became thoroughly over-excited. In London, Whistler, Wilde and Randolph Churchill hung on her words. Even Gladstone goggled. In addition to the heir to the throne, she got a yacht, a Cesarewitch winner called Merman (not, alas, Ethel), and a daughter, though Mr. Gerson's laborious researches have failed to discover which admirer it was who had effectively gone bump in the night.

For her talents as an actress, we can rely on the opinion of an expert, Ellen Terry, who saw her as Rosalind: 'The role requires the services of an actress, not those of a pretty elocutionist.' It did not matter. Both in America and England audiences flocked to see her, and who indeed, in somewhat similar circumstances, would not in the 1930s have pressed in to see Mrs. Simpson in a revival of *A Cuckoo in the Nest?*

In all this, one's heart goes out to the wretched Edward Langtry whose sole achievement on Life's Pathway was to give a surname (she was *née* Le Breton) to the statuesque celebrity. It appears that she found him uninteresting in bed. Well, it takes two to make a marital failure. Early on he resorted, and who would blame him, to stimulants, lurching repeatedly, purple and sozzled, to the sideboard, and subsequently lurching out of history via bankruptcy and the Chester County Asylum, Mrs. Langtry taking this blow courageously on the chin. They don't, I suspect, come any tougher.

FLOREAT

Forty Years On: An Anthology of School Songs, compiled by Gavin Ewart (Sidgwick & Jackson, 1969).

School Songs start with an advantage. They are sung most often at the end of term when, in the general upsurge of relief, almost anything seems acceptable. Back scrape the benches, up rise the boys, forth peals the organ. A dreadful geniality seizes the staff and, in the gallery, Matron inflates her lungs and lets fly with her rich mezzo. And here is Mr. Ewart to tell us, in splendid fullness, what they sing.

Nothing special, really. As lyrics they are no great shakes. The songs were mostly run up on the premises by local talent ('We'll strive with zest to do our best') when public schools were fast expanding in the late Victorian days. The writers were inclined to make use of unlovely words such as *guerdon, chaunt, scutcheon, lightsome* and *I ween.* Even a professional poet,

The Pleasures of Reading

Sir Henry Newbolt, could provide only sub-standard stuff for his old school, Clifton:

> For working days or holidays,
> And glad or melancholy days,
> They are great days and jolly days
> At the best School of all.

The present Poet Laureate, Cecil Day-Lewis, also caught the general style on behalf of Larchfield School:

> All that you gave our eager boyhood
> How can we hope to repay?
> For you've taught us to go straight
> When the ball is at our feet,
> And tackle any fate that comes our way.

As song writers, headmasters proved alarmingly fruitful. The record shows saintly Thring of Uppingham notching up 11, Cyril Alington bursting out into Latin for Shrewsbury, Cyril Norwood supplying Marlborough with two and then, translated to Harrow, churning out four for that already over-songed school. The horrible muse of Sunderland Lewis ('Under-hand skew-knees' to the boys) coughed up five for Haileybury, including some O.T.C. japes:

> Think of lying under canvas
> On a downy palliasse
> With no end of pally asses near.

This won't do at all. Headmasters should be far too busy to write anything. Their function is to scuttle suspiciously about, pop unexpectedly up, and uncover something unfortunate.

A careful study of the traditional Eton song shows it to be a thinly-disguised rowing manual for beginners, with its insistence on uniformity, steady rhythm, maximum leverage and the inconvenience of catching crabs. References to a hay-harvest breeze and shady trees are there to persuade the gullible that the hideous activity has its enjoyable side.

But, low though the standard is, *goodness* abounds. Roedean

Girls will be Girls

spares a thought for, it seems, an old-girl cricket team touring Borneo:

> Honour to those who in tropical suns
> Add to our laurels with runs upon runs.

Tonbridge draws attention to the difficulties of the Careers Master:

> Perish every sluggard, let us all be men,
> Choose we for Life's weapon harp or sword or pen.

Malvern College pays tribute to the deliciously uncontaminated water so near at hand, Worcestershire's defiant answer to Evian:

> Nobis sunt aeterni montes
> Quique dant salutem fontes.

Harrow, eyes modestly lowered, recalls the giants of the past:

> For all of we, whoever we be,
> Come short of the lions of old, you see.

And a bit short on grammar, too.

A mystery remains. Uppingham, a distinguished rugger-playing school, has a football song which contains these lines:

> See the madness surge and rise,
> Toes twice sixty kick the skies.

Twice 60 is 120. 120 toes between 30 players? Not enough to go round. Possibly the reference is to a term when the intake of malformed boys was unusually high.

Mr. Ewart has somewhat skimped his homework. Glosses are few. Not everybody knows the meaning of 'Bill' at Harrow. What is the 'Gutter' at Tonbridge? Of what consists the Marlborough dish called 'Bolly', and what is a 'Kish'? For these shortcomings he must be 'whopped' (Harrow) and have his tuck-box confiscated.

The Pleasures of Reading

In due course school songs will doubtless march with the times. Old boys returning are invariably 'Some from Cam and some from Isis'. Not a whiff of Redbrick, so let's make a start:

> Some their blithesome paths are treading
> From those roomy 'digs' in Reading.
> Student life can ne'er be dull
> 'Mid the fishy smells of Hull.

You see? There's nothing to it.

MARMALADE, MA'AM?

Dreams About H.M. The Queen. By Brian Masters (Blond & Briggs, 1972).
Journey into Light. By Ruth Plant (Cassell).
A Gallery of Ghosts. By Andrew Mackenzie (Arthur Barker).

I don't suppose it's at all widely known that two or three times a year I breakfast quite informally with the Queen in her Windsor boudoir. Only the two of us and everything just as snug as snug. After her All Bran and prunes, Her Majesty favours for her main dish really rather a *mound* of tinned salmon, while at the 'preserve' stage, Robertson's Golden Shred seems especially pleasing to the royal tooth. No corgis, and Prince Philip breakfasting in bed (a likely story).

Oh dear. Mr. Masters tells me that in dreaming about this delightful relationship (conversation flows, and we *roar!*), I am merely compensating for lack of glamour in my own life. To judge by the royal family dreams he has collected in this very merry book, glamour must be in short supply (even Lord Northcliffe, who had access to glamour, dreamt that he had run off with Princess Mary and they had started a boarding-house at Blackpool).

The Queen gets about much more than her subjects imagine. Occasionally she lives in an Earls Court bed-sitter or in a caravan and she is fond, almost to excess, of cups of tea. She has been seen as a plucky goal-keeper, covered in mud and a bit of a butterfingers, and she is a deft lorry-driver, perched up on a telephone directory to reach the wheel and shouting reprovingly at road-hogs. She was once found in a pub drinking her pint of bitter and, absent-mindedly, that of Prince Charles who had gone outside for a moment. If she has a fault, it is that she is prone to wear her crown on all occasions, even balancing it on her pixie-hood in inclement weather. But on the whole, whether darning socks, running up a shepherd's pie or queueing for the B.B.C. canteen, a most competent and friendly person.

The Queen Mother, on the other hand, is in constant trouble. If the Queen drops in unexpectedly for tea in Middlesbrough (wearing, naturally, her coronation dress), the Queen Mother is found lurking about outside in gum boots and looking sheepish. Clutching a plastic laundry bag, she frequently makes her sad way to a launderette in the Buckingham Palace Road. Arriving at Gatwick with twenty corgis, she loses her passport, and that is not all:

> I overheard an official say, 'I am sorry, ma'am, but you will have to stay in quarantine with the dogs. We can fix up a perfectly comfortable kennel for you for six months.' The Queen Mother looked near to tears, but resigned to take it philosophically. The next thing I remember, I saw the Queen Mother cooped up in a kennel, still wearing a nice flowered frock, and carrying her handbag.

The Queen Mother makes all her own jam but clumsily drops pot after pot ('I was worried about her enormous sequined dress becoming soiled'), and indeed her few happy moments are only when screeching in grand opera at the Albert Hall or dancing barefooted, an abandoned Isadora Duncan, in St. James's Park.

Noël Coward, *Blithe Spirit*, and particularly Margaret Rutherford as Madame Arcati, have done a hilarious disservice to the psychic world, and one's own confidence in the Other Life was anyhow pretty limited. However, if anybody can swallow it, good luck to them. *Journey into Light* is about the successful efforts of the authoress's brother, Ralph, who died forty years ago as a young man, to 'get through to us from the Unseen' with the help of a 'sensitive' called Mrs. Osborne Leonard. Everything goes swimmingly:

> Once the sitting had begun and Mrs. Osborne Leonard was in a trance, Feda, her control, came through from the Other Life and exclaimed, 'Have you been asked to help a boy? There is one here in a rush to come.'

Little Feda, of partly Indian descent, was only thirteen 'when she passed to the Other Life', is the medium 'over there', and wins all hearts by lisping, during a hitch, ' 'nt it a noosence?' Stenographer to Mrs. Osborne Leonard: Mrs. Muriel Hankey.

Little Feda, dressed in blue gauze, 'comes through' repeatedly with yells of 'Good morning good morning I come I come' while Mrs. Osborne Leonard reposes pleasantly after much stertorous breathing and acts as a human telephone operator. And there, down the wires, is Ralph, as chatty as can be ('You know, dear, I am becoming quite a centre of attraction here'). The latest news from the Hereafter is nothing but jolly. New bodies are provided and, on Ralph's father's demise, he gets his old teeth back again and advises his daughter to join the London School of Economics. Both have visited the 'Christ Sphere' and made bags of new friends.

After retirement to a vegetarian guest house, Mrs. Osborne Leonard herself passed across in 1968 but passed fairly swiftly back again accompanied by Sir Oliver Lodge.

One thing worries me. Mrs. Osborne Leonard is described as 'a professional' but nowhere is there any mention of her fees. What were they? Were there reductions for off-peak periods? Was she paid by results or per trance? If she failed to get through ('I am trying to connect you'), were the fees deductible? My own guess is that she managed to get through really quite often.

I have had occasion before to complain of the selfish and listless behaviour of ghosts. Why return at all if they aren't going to contribute? I now complain again. None of the apparitions in Mr. Mackenzie's splendid gleanings from autobiographies are the faintest use. Ghosts stand immobile on staircases, they upset residents in Cheltenham, they wear squeaky boots, they wink alarmingly, they wring their hands, they play accordions, they glide through closed doors, they remove their heads and make disagreeable smells. One of the most irritating dresses in white satin, sits on a plough and gazes at the moon. Perhaps it's Mrs. Osborne Leonard.

HE, SHE AND IT

Elinor Glyn. By Anthony Glyn (Hutchinson, 1955).

Psycho-analysts, digging about in this immensely enjoyable and well written biography of the creator of 'It', will soon unearth possible reasons for Elinor Glyn's heavy bias towards the romantic and highly coloured in her numerous novels.

Repressed in her youth and told that the display of emotion was 'servants' behaviour', she was further discouraged by the information that she was ugly. Experience rapidly proved this excitingly false. A young Etonian gave her a peck in Jersey, and on a visit to the Paris Zoo a Frenchman repeatedly hissed *'belle tigresse!'* into her ear. Soon, proposals of marriage came pouring in, from a bibulous and be-walrused peer, a bearded millionaire and the Duke of Newcastle. She settled for a rich and amiable Essex landowner, Clayton Glyn, who wafted her into the *beau monde* and the country-house life which she was so faithfully to reproduce in those of her books which required accuracy upon these points. Mr. Glyn enlivened the Brighton honeymoon by hiring the public baths, in which the green-eyed bride swam slowly up and down, concealed by nothing but her long, red hair.

With that gesture, Mr. Glyn's romantic bolt was shot, but other, virtuous admirers were not lacking. There was Major Seymour Wynne Finch, in a Paisley shawl smoking suit, and Prince Gritzo Wittgenstein, who clasped her so close in a waltz that his Cossack cross-belts left red weals on her exposed portions. Lord Milner read Plato to her on terraces, and Lord

The Pleasures of Reading

Curzon did the same with Aristotle. With Lord Alastair Innes-Ker she admired the palace of Versailles ('Gosh! What a lot of lightning conductors'!), and there was a Mr. Van Allen, with whom the Glyns and their maid, Williams, made the best of crowded accommodation in Naples:

> Williams was appalled at the presumption of sharing a bed with her mistress and slept on the very edge. Clayton and Mr. Van Allen undressed with difficulty behind a small screen. It was a disturbed night. The valet sat bolt upright on a small gilt chair, his mouth wide open, snoring hard, while his master occasionally shouted at him. At intervals Williams fell out of bed. The lamplight poured into the room through the Venetian blinds and when Elinor sat up in bed to get a breath of air, she noticed Mr. Van Allen, propped up on one elbow, murmuring 'God! What a form!'

Clayton's comment next day was characteristic: 'Old fool! Bothering about women when we were all so tired.'

But whatever romance was missing in her home life, Mrs. Glyn made up for on the printed page. Her heroines had the knack of marrying well, hooking, between them, two dukes, a marquis and an earl, three barons, five baronets, a Scottish laird and a sprinkling of titled foreign fry. The women's names were on the unusual side: Zara Shulski, Morella Winmarleigh, Guinevere Bohun, Ethelfrida Montfichet, Halcyone La Sarthe, Sabine Delburg, Vanessa St. Austell. Unusual, too, was their behaviour:

> They were sitting on the tiger by now, and she undulated round and all over him, feeling his coat, and his face, and his hair, as a blind person might, till at last it seemed as if she were twined about him like a serpent.

The tiger was a skinned one, and the book is *Three Weeks*, the writing of which, in 1906, caused little difficulty ('It seemed as though some spirit from beyond was guiding me'). Reviewers were in little doubt whence the spirit came and publication caused a rumpus: 'A mawkish display of sickly sentimentalism'; 'Lack of delicacy and refinement'. However, appreciative

Girls will be Girls

letters came from Australian bushmen, Klondike miners and Roman Catholic priests, and Lords Curzon and Milner sent tiger-skins. The sales of this book alone went into millions, which was satisfactory, Mr. Glyn having been living on capital, and his wife, without complaint, now finding herself supporting the whole family.

Mr. Anthony Glyn, the subject's grandson, has produced a fascinating and extremely amusing record. Good things abound. Mrs. Glyn's beauty was bolstered by 'the secret treatment of El Zair', scrubbing the face with a dry nailbrush, and sleeping with the feet to the magnetic north ('pure common sense'). She visited Mrs. Vanderbilt and found her knee-deep in footmen and with the chamber pots tastefully concealed by lace covers. And Mrs. Glyn had a novel way with Income Tax demands ('she tended to ignore them, vaguely thinking them unjust').

Where, on her particular literary ladder, should Elinor Glyn be placed? Perhaps level with Marie Corelli, with Ouida a rung or two below, and Ethel M. Dell gamely beginning the ascent. Of her own abilities and worth she took a modest view. Speaking, in 1931, at an International P.E.N. congress in Europe, she said:

> I write about rich environments, and lovely women and handsome men and perfect love, and a lot about beautiful babies for those who can never have any. It isn't a bit clever, but people do seem to like it.

CHRISTMAS REVIEWS OF BOOKS FOR GIRLS

1959

I SAY—THANKS AWFULLY!

Trials for the Chalet School. By Elinor Brent-Dyer (Chambers).
Emperor of Space. By Tom Allum (Blackie).
The Lark in the Morn. By Elfrida Vipont (Oxford University Press).

Trials for the Chalet School finds Miss Brent-Dyer in really spanking form and with girls as bizarrely named as ever—Emerence Hope, Zita Rincini, Amandine Robinet, Prudence Dawbarn, Blossom Willoughby and Verity Carey (a mezzo-soprano with gentian eyes). Prominent among the trials is a new girl, Naomi Elton, who is crippled and 'warped' ('My people were agnostics, I believe'). In class she corrects 'a light misquotation of the Head's with a suave certainty' and resents Jocelyn Fawcett's merry chatter:

> 'I had no idea', she said icily, 'that in a school where the girls were *supposed* to be gentlewomen—at least, I imagine so—people would be so totally incapable of anything approaching real conversation.'

Attempts are made to cheer poor Naomi up ('Squat on our toboggan') but after meeting the art master ('You speak German, hein?') she comes a cropper on the ice and conks completely out. Barely recovered, she is cheered up again ('Who will tow Naomi?') before being nearly swept away by an avalanche (see generously coloured jacket). Even in the final pages of the book, she is hurled out of a motor-bicycle combination and fetches up against a boulder. So much for agnosticism.

Girls will be Girls

The Chalet School has an unusual Mademoiselle (*'Eh bien, mes petites'*) who zooms about on skis wearing bright red and has even been spotted careering down the Cresta. *How* Miss Brazil would have frowned! Matron is reliability itself when Margot, in Pansy dorm, gets delirious ('Scarlet, I'm afraid') and takes temps all round. Mary-Lou Trelawny is now Head Girl ('Take over, Vi, will you?') and her eyes 'glint like pieces of steel' when pranksome juniors stuff the Lost Property cupboard with pilfered possessions—Lesley Bethune's snap-album, Vi's Tennis Six badge, Miss Farrars' map-case ('awfully nifty'), Richenda Fry's umbrella, and Matron's reading-glass ('Whoever did this must have been at my drawers'). The ring-leader is Aline Russell (Lady Russell's girl, you know) and the discovered culprits 'weep like waterspouts' (poor little Tessa de Barsac is particularly drenched).

In *Emperor of Space*, Guy Abbott, fifteen-year-old president of his school astronautical society, is lucky enough to meet Professor Julian Harvey who has 'an air of breeding' and a home-made, unlicensed, electro-magnetic space-ship ('Professor, this is simply terrific'), in a hangar in his garden. The arrival of four escaping convicts settles the crew problem and, at pistol-point, they are pressed into service (' "Enter!", the Professor ordered hysterically'). In two twos the contraption is soaring away ('Frankly, its efficiency surprised me') towards the planet Imperator. Speed: 25,000 m.p.h. Food: tins containing 'a balanced meal rendered to a thick paste with gelatine'. The pince-nezed Professor ('Goodbye for now') becomes slightly deranged at take-off and the convicts are nothing but cross-patches. A meteor ('Gosh, a meteor!') nearly hits them, but the landing on Imperator is safely accomplished ('Remain calm, everyone'), the Professor 'deftly flicking the locking pin from the handwheel hub'. Vegetation on Imperator is lobed and comes in delicate pastel shades. Warning everybody to beware of strange smells, the gifted savant steps out, only to fall flat, dead as a doornail. Can Guy, with the smoothing rectifier dented, pilot the space-ship? 'I'll try, but honestly I think it's beyond me.'

Meanwhile, Dr. Harold Emsworth's rocket-ship has also landed. Speed: 'exceptional'. Food: porridge, cocoa, lamb chops.

Christmas Reviews of Books for Girls: 1959 and 1961

Traitor: kindly supplied by the Ministry of Fuel and Power. Radio contact is made with the earth ('Your parents are well') and the party takes a stroll ('We'll travel openly, chatting as the fancy takes us'). The return journey ('He moved the vertical lever one notch of the ratchet in the plus direction') presents no difficulties, and there are Mum and Dad on the landing-strip ('Pity you couldn't have had your hair cut').

Lark in the Morn brings us to Heryot Friends' School, where Sylvia Felpham is simply topping to Kit Haverard ('I say—thanks awfully'). There are two music mistresses, Miss Fishwick, who is aquiline-nosed and has Beethoven's death-mask over her upright, and Miss Tattersall who, despite training by Madame Cantelina herself, is far too inclined to slop about in 'a négligée of petunia-coloured silk and feather-trimmed mules to match'. The great Simon Trent ('simply divine') comes down to sing, and Kit, dead nuts on music, is permitted to explore his rib-cage and diaphragm. Tattersall (Fishwick has 'flu) accompanies him, getting flustered at rehearsal ('We'll start with the Scarlatti. I'm not going to sing out'). At the concert, Tatty goes to pieces, contributing in the trickier passages one note per bar, but sharply recovers her aplomb ('Let's all have a chocolate'). Simon Trent, a keen gargler, appears again at a charity concert (floods in West China), bringing with him Rudolf Brenner ('You like my playing, hein?') and his 'priceless Strad', but this time Old Fish is at the ivories ('Would you care to turn over for me? I haven't had a good turner-over since Sylvia Felpham left'). Is there, you are wondering, an attempt on Herr Brenner's valuable instrument? But of course, foiled by Kit, who subsequently warbles her way into everybody's heart, in front of Sir Geoffrey Chauntesinger too, at yet another charity concert (earthquake in India).

Girls will be Girls

CHRISTMAS REVIEWS OF BOOKS FOR GIRLS

1961

JOICKS

Young Netball Player. By Jacynth Hope-Simpson (Constable).
Reindeer Girl. By Margaret Ruthin (Dobson).
The Fourth Was Fun for Philippa. By Nancy Breary (Blackie).
Bob-a-Job Pony. By Olive Norton (Heinemann).
Moon Base One. By Hugh Walters (Faber).

Who can say that authoresses of school stories don't move with the times? In *Young Netball Player*, flooded hockey grounds cause Mrs. Symonds to concentrate on invigorating netball and Liz shoots seven goals (' "Just a knack", said Liz, grinning'). A natural games player is Amanda Jackson from Jamaica ('quite the laziest girl we have ever had in the school') who complains of the cold, plays in enormous brown fur gloves, and goes on outings ('I'm taking Manda along to the launderette'). Comes the netball tournament, when all depends on rattling Manda into activity. In the opening game against the Ladies' Netball Club, supercilious onlookers satisfactorily enrage the dusky player:

> Manda clearly was not amused. Her large eyes were rolling. Her hair, which after a great deal of trouble, she had made nearly straight, had burst out of its ribbon and was crackling.

Astute little Caroline wonders what she can say to get the coloured girl's goat really up. Ah, happy thought!

> 'Manda, these people are segregationalists. They support *apartheid*. They believe that whites are better than blacks. The West Indies depends on *you*.'
> Manda hissed, and the breath came out of her nostrils as clouds of hot steam in the cold winter air.

Christmas Reviews of Books for Girls: 1959 and 1961

One would hardly have cared to be selected for the Ladies, and Manda's gyrations also make mincemeat of the Youth Club (black jeans, broderie anglaise blouses, and imitation-suede jerkins). And so to the Final, against snooty Halford House (gold, maroon and olive green) and another triumph, with Manda 'zigzagging like an electric current'. As for June— 'her knees were dripping with blood and her shirt had come out of her shorts'. The sporting limelight has the worst effect on Manda. She is sent to Miss Lloyd for talking during prayers, and makes a speedy return visit for using insulting language during a history lesson about Nelson. She seems only really happy at a sewing-machine. *Too* revealing, my dear.

There is something engaging (Santa, and all that) about reindeer but fully to enjoy *Reindeer Girl* it would be helpful to have a real thing about reindeer. Little Elli had known no home but a Lapp tent and no companions but nut-brown Grandmother Kirsti, Grandfather Jussa, Brother Johan, and approximately three hundred reindeer. The Lapp *cuisine* is limited (reindeer sausages, bread, fried reindeer, dried reindeer, more bread, grilled reindeer, birch tea and snow) but there is abundant bird life, with the snow ptarmigan (G-bek . . . g-bek . . . g-bek . . .), golden plover (Peep . . . peep . . . peep . . .), black-cock (Soohee . . . soohee . . . soohee . . .) and an occasional Siberian tit. You'll want to know how to summon reindeer (Aw . . . aw . . . aw . . .) and what *they* live on (Reindeer moss).

Elli turns out to be an heiress and attempts are made to helicopter her to Helsingfors, but she is happier in her *peske*, riding on her *pulka* and stuffing sweet-scented senna grass into her *skaller*. Even Elli's birthmark comes in a stag antler design. Grandmother Kirsti, however, has broader ideas and puts them into extempore local song:

> She started to *joick*. It was long since she had *joicked*. . . . She *joicked* a last verse.
>
> > Herd must vanish, Elli too,
> > Nun-nun-nuu, nun-nun-nuu,
> > In Russki land we'll start anew,
> > Nun-nun-nuu, nun-nun-nuu.

Girls will be Girls

Now, now, now!

The Fourth Was Fun for Philippa begins delightfully with the whole of the check-ginghamed Lower Fourth plunging, screaming, into a pond from a collapsed pseudo-Japanese ornamental bridge ('a very costly work of art'). A massive, uniformed Matron is soon on the scene and subsequently 'submerges' Louella under an electric hair-drier ('a cheerful, wholesome expression is more attractive than a lot of curled-up hair'). The Headmistress, Miss Bonnerille, is given to 'sly digs in a foreign language' and is very go-ahead: besides the hair-drier, there are weekly Canasta matches, French crosswords, hardly any games, and punishments consist of duster-hemming for the Cathedral Fabric Fund. The head girl, Elsa Brett (Second Prefect: Domini Halstead), is stingy with extra blotting-paper and inclined to 'too much nervous self-pity', a condition aggravated by a new girl, Philippa Dene, who arrives in a mauve travelling-suit and briskly accuses Elsa of having bitten her elder sister, Nerissa, on the knee ('the remark spelled cheek').

The book is crammed with refreshing incidents—there is an explosion at the pumping-station, Philippa falls into a hollow tree-trunk ('she is being returned to school on the fire-engine'), homesick Charlotte blubs and Melanie calms her with chocs, Louella is arrested by the police, Philippa's violet earrings are 'practically snatched from her ears by Matron', and there are smothered giggles from cubicles (cubicle furniture specially designed by Miss Bonnerille herself).

Bob-a-Job Pony deals with the efforts of Tabitha Graham to raise enough cash to purchase Peggy, a pony bought by the M.F.H. for his daughter, June Blennerhasset (aged 18 and already a martyr to the fragrant weed). To know Peggy is to love her—big, dark eyes, sensitive withers, gold satin coat, long, pale eyelashes, which she flutters quite a bit, and though at 14.1 she is 'not acceptable in the Register', she shows her good taste by throwing June Blennerhasset, emerald green shirt, lipstick, fags and all.

In between mucking out Thunderbolt's loose-box in tartan slacks and wisping Peggy over, there are other diversions: milking ('Squeeze as you go down, and then sort of slide to the top again. Don't let go'), and a new cow to be named ('Should it be Thelma, after Mother?'). Tabby, with her chum, Ian, formerly 'leading contralto' in the choir, takes part in a B.B.C. TV Quiz ('Sit you down there'), vanquishing a disagreeable boy in a Colin Wilson sweater who's never even heard of Asshurbanipal. Tabitha scores heavily on curry combs and Ian appears to know about Vitamin D and how to make *Maître d' Hôtel* butter ('Mother thinks it's a good idea for chaps to be able to cook'). Hm! Then Tabby's sister, Anna-Jane, falls into the swollen river, bobbing about like a Hallowe'en apple ('Mother got cracking with artificial respiration'), but recovers sufficiently to be able to knock out a burglar with a shillelagh. Can it be the dreaded 'Gipsy' Warwick (£1,000 reward)? No, alas; just a nonentity of no fixed address. Tch! Never mind, everything turns out splendidly, Peggy astounding one and all by suddenly producing a golden foal (with 'damp legs').

The expedition to *Moon Base One* is an international affair consisting of Chris Godfrey, crew-cut Morrison Kant, and Serge Smyslov ('Morrey, this is Serge. Serge, I want you to meet Morrey'). Morrey and Chris are, naturally, gayer than Serge, and Chris is put in command ('Er—thank you, sir'). Young and sickly Tony Hale joins the party. His mysterious illness may lead to anti-social acts ('If the boy proves at all troublesome, he must be anaesthetized') but he soon gets the hang of things:

> 'Why does the rocket have to break up into parts?' he asked.
> 'Because it's best to get rid of useless weight as soon as possible,' his friend explained, delighted at the intelligent interest the boy was showing.

Training begins on the Black Sea coast in a capsule undergoing force five 'g' as it zooms up and down a (disused) mineshaft six miles deep ('If anything goes wrong, you can ring the alarm'). Shortly after blast-off ('Everybody comfortable?'), Tony has to be reprimanded for pinching chocolate. The Moon landing ('THUD!!!') goes according to plan and the travellers erect a homey plastic dome in a convenient craterlet. Then Tony, crammed with nut-milk, goes generally to the bad but

Girls will be Girls

reforms in time to solder a broken wire ('Gone was the gloomy, sullen boy') and make the return journey possible. None of the others can solder, not even Serge. I do see that in a complicated training programme, Something Has To Go.